Homework –
Build Words –
begin

at

June 72
Psychology Today

Check finished 55 pages

TALK with your HANDS

TALK WITH

YOUR HANDS

WRITTEN AND ILLUSTRATED BY

David O. Watson

Winneconne, Wisconsin

First Printing January 1964

Reprintings:
April 1965
August 1966
May 1967
February 1968
October 1968
April 1969
November 1969
September 1970
January 1971
September 1971
January 1972

Available from the author and publisher
Winneconne, Wisconsin 54986

Printed and Bound by
GEORGE BANTA COMPANY, INC.
Menasha, Wisconsin

PRINTED IN THE UNITED STATES OF AMERICA

Foreword

Signs and gestures of one kind or another have been used since the beginning of time as a means of communication, to give emphasis to the spoken word, or to express a thought or feeling where the spoken word is found wanting.

An infant cries to attract attention, and he also kicks and waves his arms and smiles or frowns. When persons who speak different languages are drawn together they resort to gestures with their hands. In sports contests and dramatic performances instructions and signals are given by hand. On a signal from a coach, a baseball player attempts to steal a base and the umpire shows by gesture whether he is "safe" or "out." Dogs in the motion pictures are put through their paces by hand signals, for an audible command would find its way on to the sound track. There is a sign language even in nature, understood by both animals and men. A black cloud in the sky may be a "sign of rain."

So signs are a universal language. The American Indians used a highly developed system of signs. The deaf use a still more highly developed system, which is a language in itself. This book presents the sign language used by the deaf of America. It was originally brought to the United States from France, since education of the deaf in America originally was based upon the methods employed in France.

The deaf of this country are educated and well able to converse in the English language. Many are good lipreaders and they possess intelligible if not completely natural speech, but the sign language is the language they use most commonly in conversation among themselves, in their church services and in their parliamentary deliberations, because it is the most fluent means of communication for them. They appreciate it when their relatives and friends learn to use it, and talk to them on their hands.

Mr. Watson is well qualified to compile a book on the sign language. A son of deaf parents, he has used the sign language all his life. In this book he has devised a method of presentation which comes closest of any yet published to teach the reader to form the signs correctly and accurately. The best way to learn the sign language, of course, is to become acquainted with persons who use it and "learn by doing," but this book will provide an excellent foundation for any beginner, or for anyone who is not in constant association with the deaf.

Even those who are not in position to converse with the deaf will find it interesting. It will give them an additional means of communication which they will enjoy using, just for the fun of it.

BYRON B. BURNES, Litt. D.
President Emeritus, National
Association of the Deaf.

Berkeley, California,
September 9, 1963.

CONTENTS

Introduction

The language of signs is a beautiful, graceful, and expressive art of communication. It is probably the easiest of the "foreign" languages to learn. The sky is the limit as to what the eloquence of your hands can do for you, once you have mastered the signs, in communicating your thoughts to another person (or an audience of many persons) fluently and meaningfully. It provides the "break-through" in its magical power to bring members of the family, relatives, and friends closer together. As exchanged thoughts are understood there also glow undestanding, love, joy, and fellowship.

There has been a long, urgent need for a book which would make it simple for anyone to learn to use the language of the signs. For this reason this book was designed in an entirely new presentation, executed in the simplest and most direct method of pictorial line drawing, so that the "arrested" motion in print can be learned with a glance, understood and repeated by anyone who knows nothing about the signs.

Before attempting to learn the signs, the reader is advised to begin by learning the manual alphabet (or fingerspelling) as presented on page 185. Here you will find complete instruction on how to form the letters on your hand. The drawings were prepared in two different views, to make it easier to master them. You will soon be able to fingerspell words and phrases rapidly and accurately. The reader will also observe throughout the book many words spelled out on the fingers. Many words have no known signs to designate them. They are presented to show how they can be used in combination with other signs to form phrases or sentences.

Samples of conversational sign language are used in the last part of our book, featured by a few of our own make-believe characters in adventurous comical situations. It is believed this is the first attempt ever made to illustrate in the printed form conversation as normally used by deaf persons everywhere. They also show how a correct English sequence can be used in sign conversation.

It is hoped that a better understanding between the general public and the deaf can be generated from this book. The signs shown here can be used in any situation in life. Deaf children will value the book as a textbook and their most prized possession. Relatives, friends, students, seminarians, priests, pastors, and welfare workers will likewise gain from it.

During the course of preparing this book, it was my privilege to come into contact with many persons including educators and deaf leaders, and I am thankful to them all, who displayed a helpful interest. Among them I feel that I must mention Dr. Elizabeth Benson, Dean of Women at Gallaudet College, a noted authority on the sign language, and Mr. John A. Gough, Director of Captioned Films for the Deaf in the U.S. Office of Education.

Dr. David Peikoff, Director of the Gallaudet College Centennial Fund offered advice and encouragement which were an inspiration to me through many difficult hours. Mrs. Renee Roles, Office Manager in the office of the National Association of the Deaf, rendered valuable assistance in typing and preparing the material.

I am especially grateful and indebted to my old friend, Dr. Byron B. Burnes, President of the National Association of the Deaf, for help with the organization of the material. He examined the original drawings on numerous occasions, offering helpful criticism, and he assisted with the preparation of the captions. His wife, Caroline H. Burnes, also contributed many valuable suggestions, which I appreciate.

Finally, my heartfelt thanks are hereby expressed to my sister, Angela Watson, whose encouragement, enthusiasm, and faith kept me going when at times the task seemed overwhelming; and to my wife, Beatrice, and our children, David P., Starr Lea, Arthur T., and Tracy Ann, who were denied certain pleasures and were at times practically abandoned while I confined my efforts to the completion of this book.

DAVID O. WATSON

HOW TO READ, UNDERSTAND, AND REPEAT THE "ARRESTED" MOTION IN PRINT

There are a few "keys" to remember before the reader starts flipping through these pages. Most important of all is to watch the position of the hands (1). Compare your hands with the drawing. The dotted hand is your first position before the movement begins.

The movement or direction of the hand (or hands) is indicated by the red line (2). The solid red arrow (3) means only one motion is required. Thus, the card dealer deals only once if one card is asked for. The open-faced or three-sided arrow (4) indicates the motion is to be repeated two or three times . . . several cards are dealt.

PLAYING CARDS

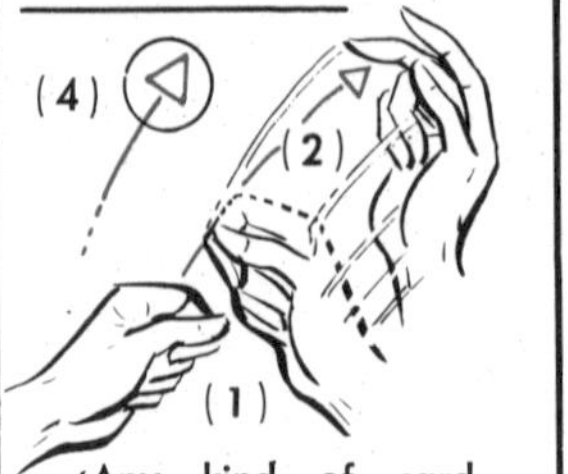

(Any kind of card game is indicated by the motion of dealing the cards.)

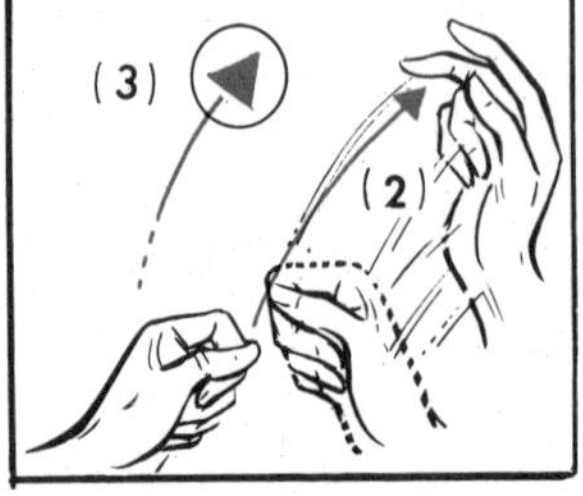

Compare the two illustrations below. The little finger dipping in the closed hand represents a brush or pen in an inkwell. Next, as seen here by the red line and solid red arrow, the hand is brought up to the "sketch pad". This is followed with a few strokes with the little finger on the "pad" as indicated by the open-faced arrow.

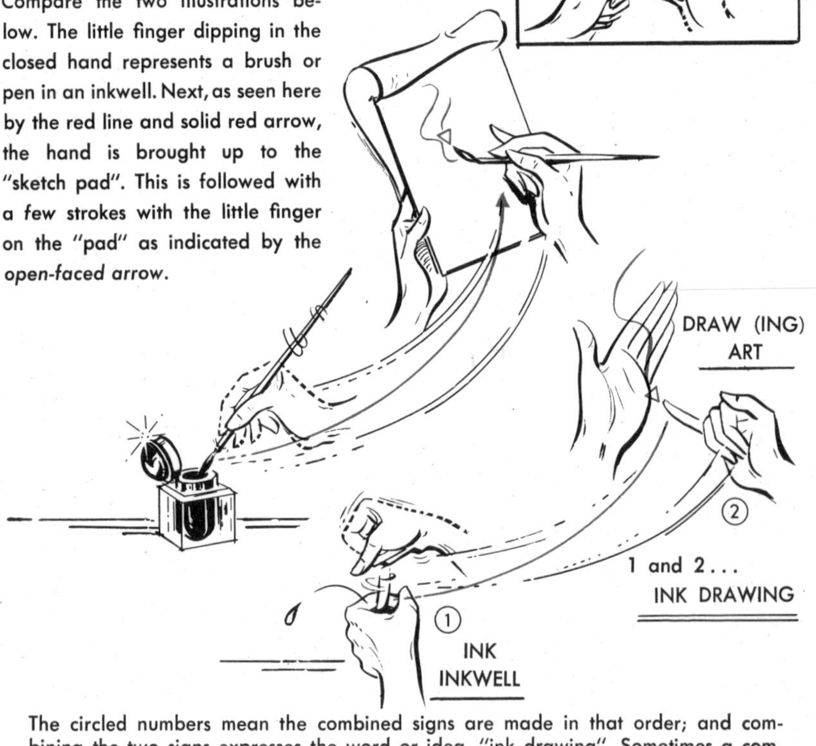

DRAW (ING) ART

1 and 2 . . .
INK DRAWING

INK
INKWELL

The circled numbers mean the combined signs are made in that order; and combining the two signs expresses the word or idea, "ink drawing". Sometimes a combination of three signs is formed to express an idea.

PERSONAL
RELATIVE
AND
INDEFINITE
PRONOUNS

I

ME
This sign is also
used to indicate
"I"

YOU

MY
MINE

① ②
HE

③ ④
SHE

YOUR
YOURS,

1 and 5 ...
3 and 5 ...
THEY
⑤

THEIR
(or YOUR, denoting
more than one person)

1

WHO

WHOSE
A combination of
WHO and YOUR
(possessive).

OUR

US- U Hand

WE   W Hand

OURSELVES

MYSELF,

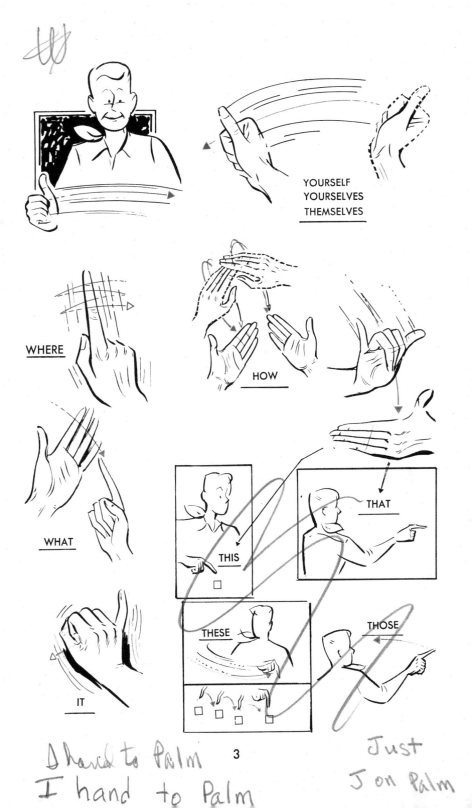

YOURSELF
YOURSELVES
THEMSELVES

WHERE

HOW

WHAT

THIS

THAT

THESE

THOSE

IT

3

D hand to Palm
I hand to Palm

Just
J on Palm

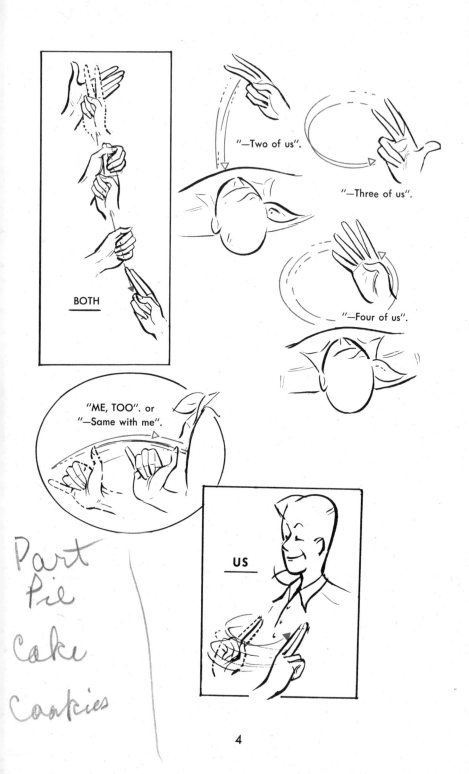

"—Two of us".

"—Three of us".

"—Four of us".

BOTH

"ME, TOO". or
"—Same with me".

US

Part
Pie
Cake
Cookies

4

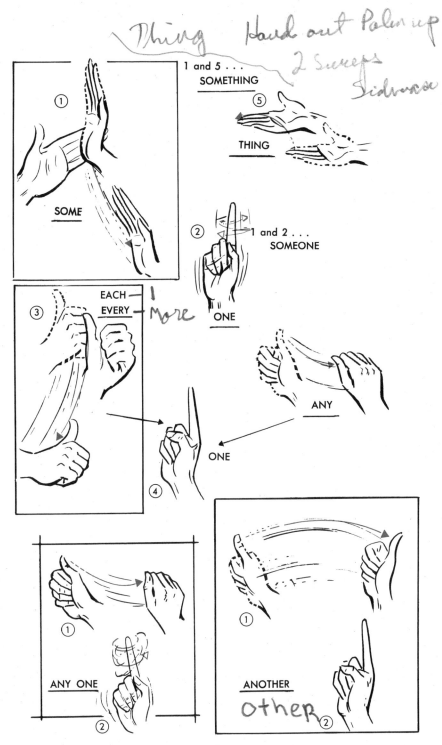

Thing   Hand out Palm up
         2 Sweeps
              Sidwase

1 and 5 . . .
SOMETHING

⑤

THING

① SOME

② 1 and 2 . . .
SOMEONE

ONE

③ EACH
EVERY   More

ANY

ONE

④

ANY ONE

①
②

ANOTHER
Other
①
②

5

Be - B Hand From Lips

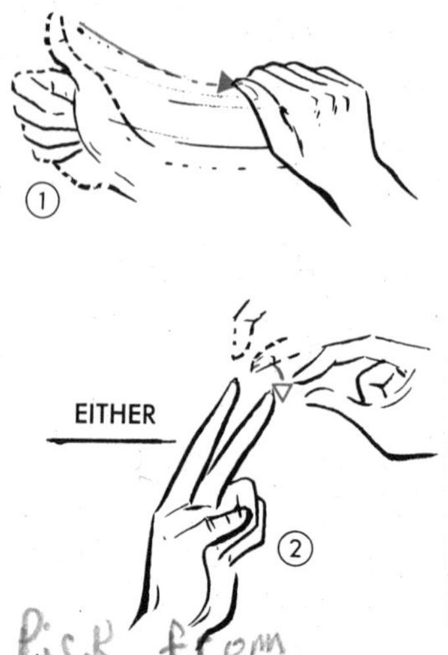

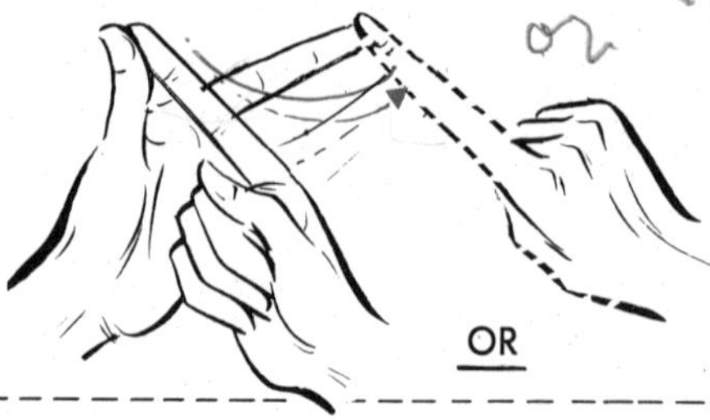

either or

①

OR

EITHER

②

Who's that? ①

②

pick from

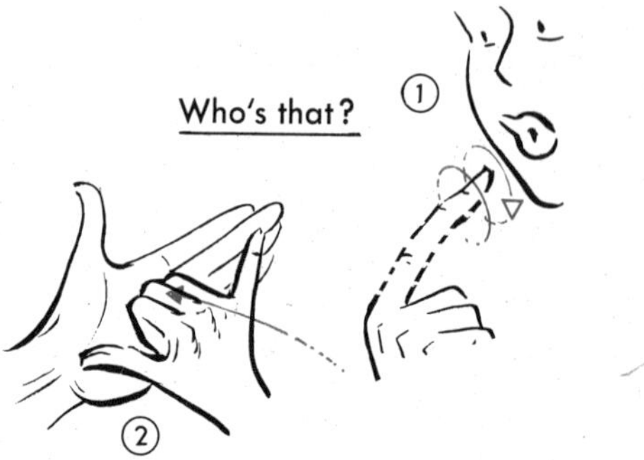

NEITHER

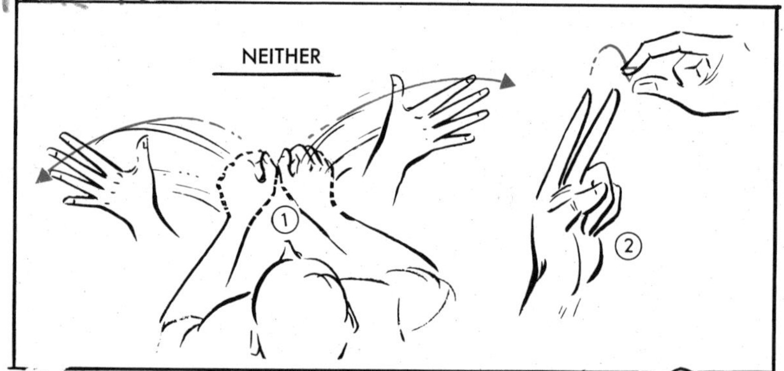

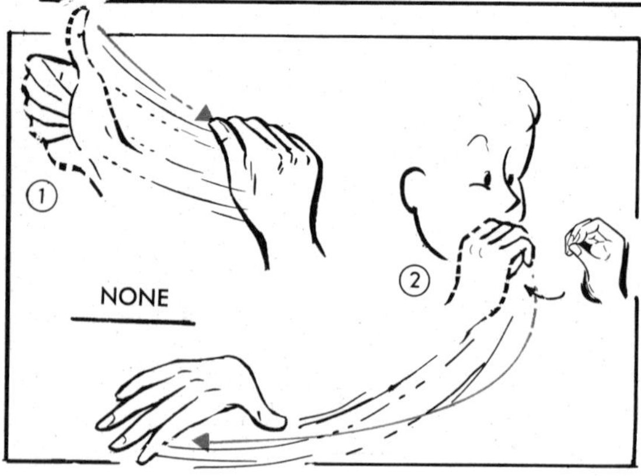

①

②

NONE

①

②

ONE ANOTHER

Sign them

Sign

6

PREPOSITIONS
AND
CONJUNCTIONS

EXCEPT

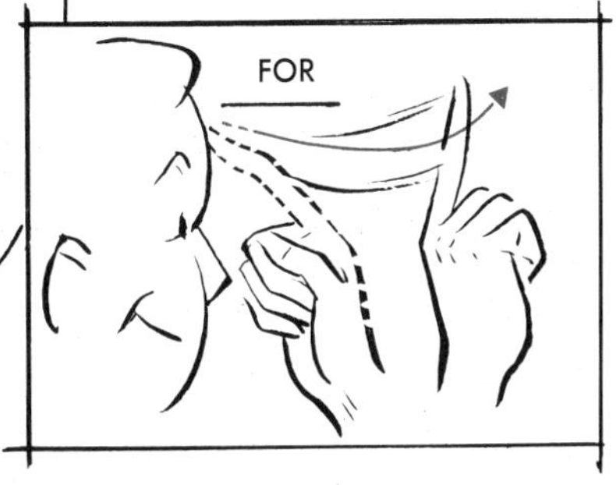

FOR

IN
INTO

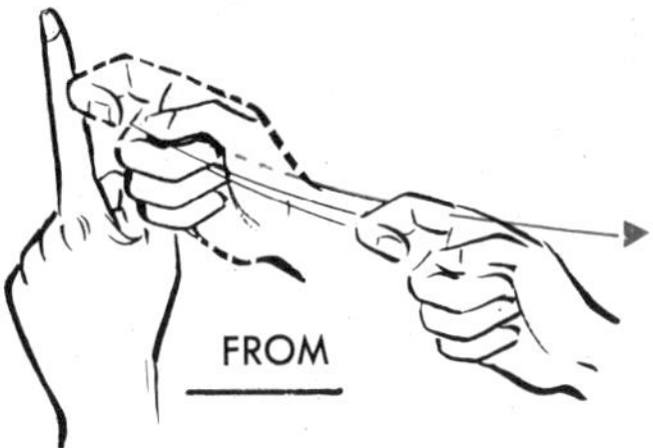

FROM

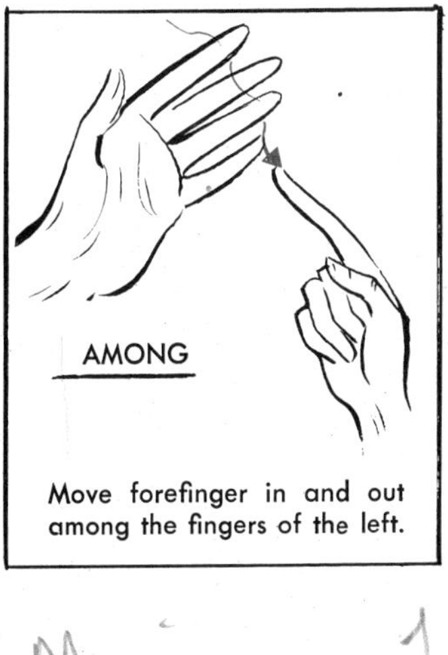

MOREOVER
BESIDE

AMONG

Move forefinger in and out among the fingers of the left.

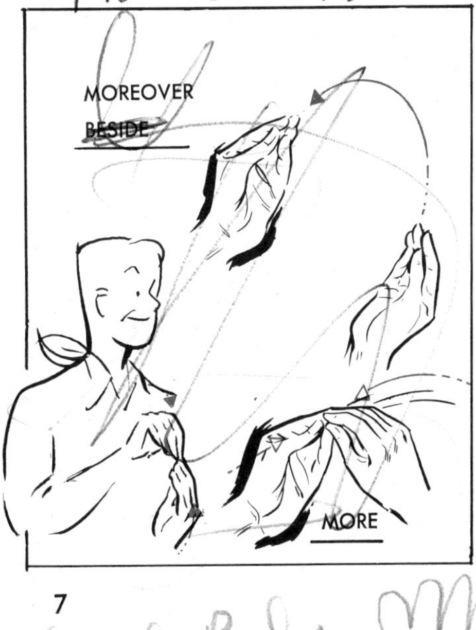

MORE

7

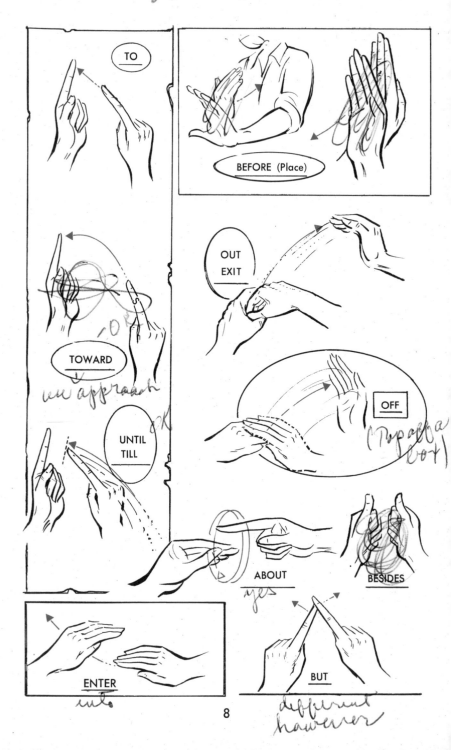

TO

BEFORE (Place)

OUT
EXIT

TOWARD

OFF

UNTIL
TILL

ABOUT

BESIDES

ENTER

BUT

8

Papers - more than 1

Close - or Beside

WITH (or BESIDE)
WITHOUT
TOGETHER (accompany)
goes away
higher than
BELOW
ABOVE
ABOVE
BELOW
lower than
ON (UPON)
GONE
"FADE AWAY"
DEPLETED ("All gone")

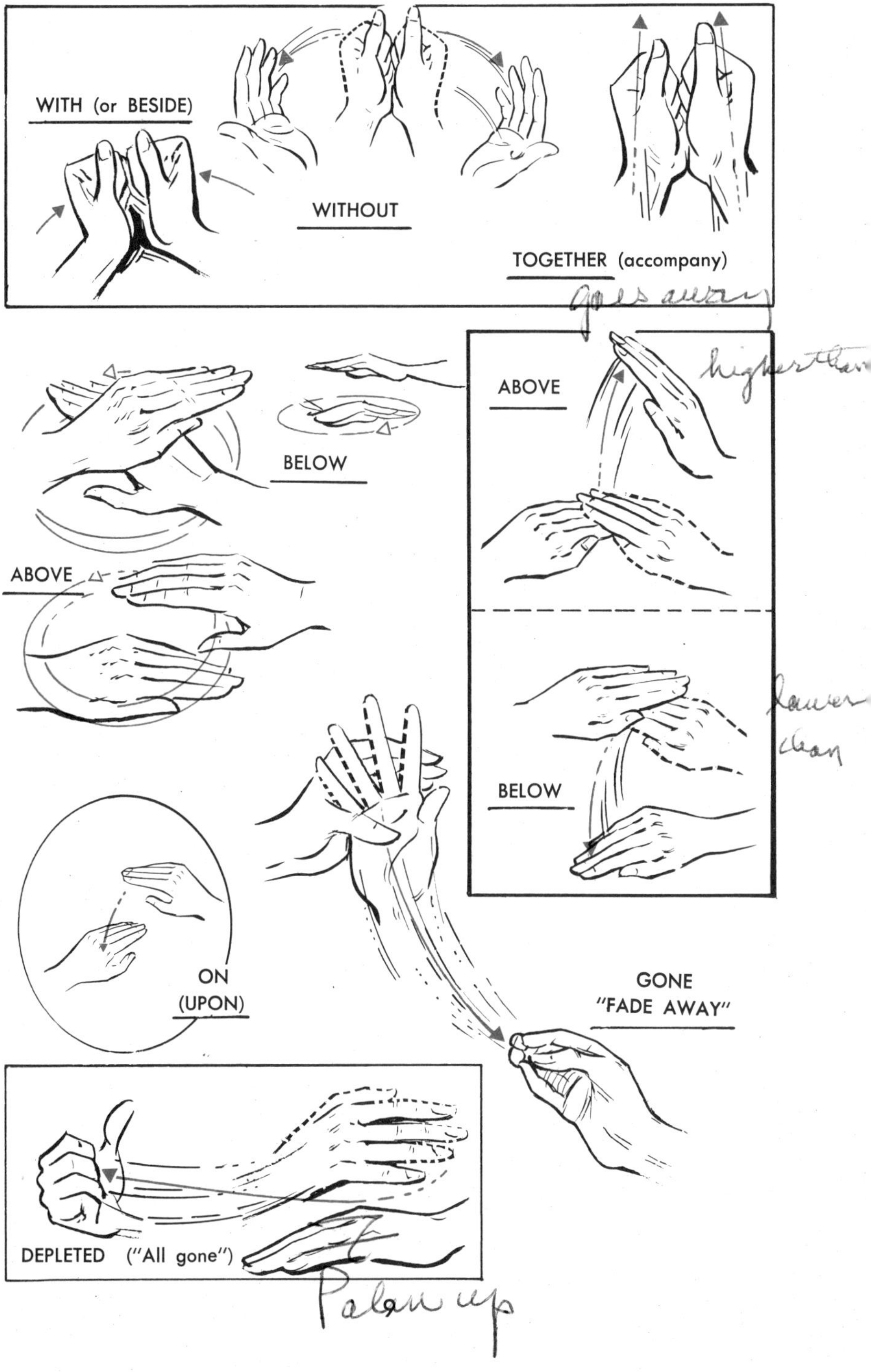

Palm up

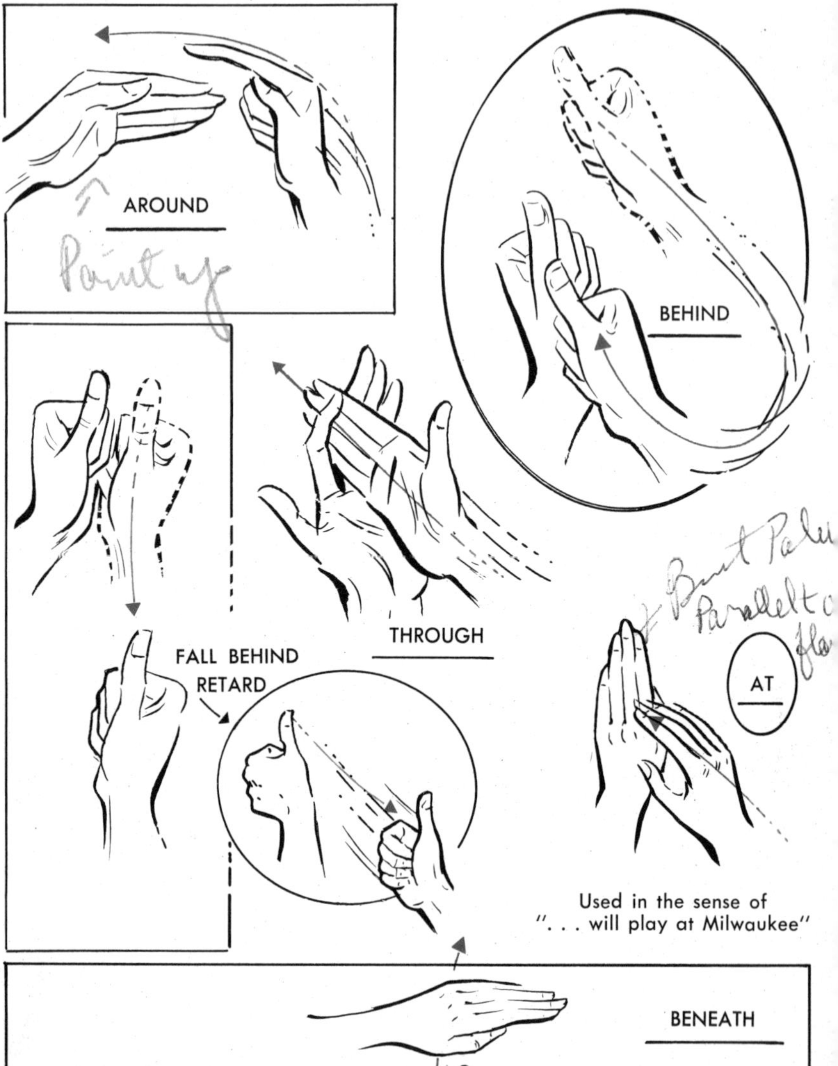

AROUND

BEHIND

THROUGH

FALL BEHIND
RETARD

AT

Used in the sense of
". . . will play at Milwaukee"

BENEATH

UNDERNEATH

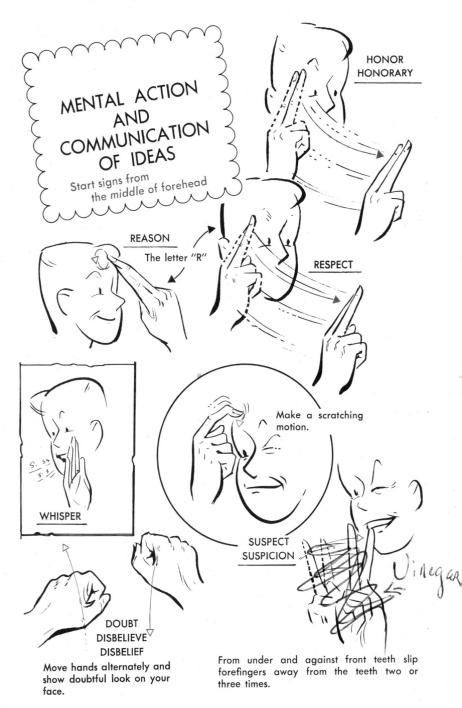

MENTAL ACTION AND COMMUNICATION OF IDEAS

Start signs from the middle of forehead

HONOR
HONORARY

REASON
The letter "R"

RESPECT

Make a scratching motion.

WHISPER

SUSPECT
SUSPICION

DOUBT
DISBELIEVE
DISBELIEF

Move hands alternately and show doubtful look on your face.

From under and against front teeth slip forefingers away from the teeth two or three times.

11

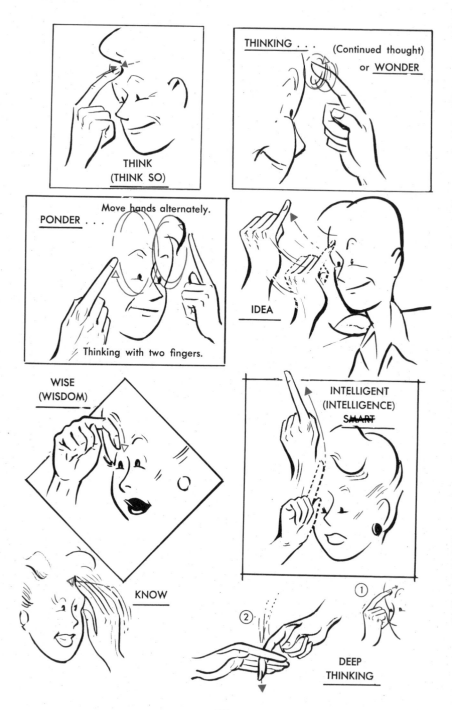

THINK
(THINK SO)

THINKING . . . (Continued thought)
or WONDER

PONDER . . .
Move hands alternately.
Thinking with two fingers.

IDEA

WISE
(WISDOM)

INTELLIGENT
(INTELLIGENCE)
SMART

KNOW

DEEP
THINKING

12

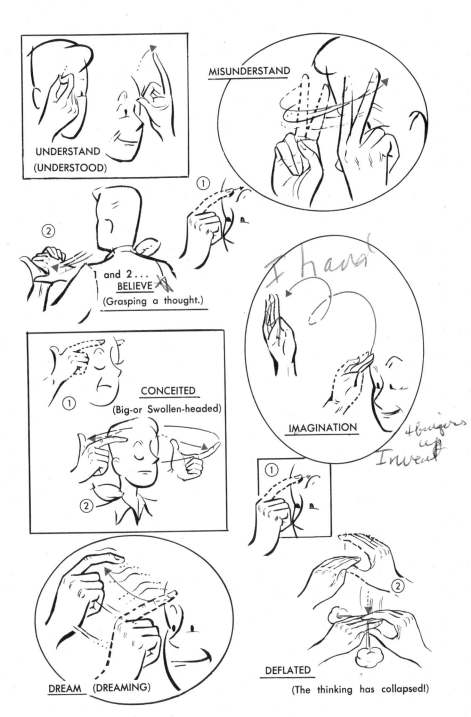

UNDERSTAND
(UNDERSTOOD)

MISUNDERSTAND

① ②
1 and 2 . . .
BELIEVE
(Grasping a thought.)

CONCEITED
(Big-or Swollen-headed)
①
②

IMAGINATION

①
②
DEFLATED
(The thinking has collapsed!)

DREAM (DREAMING)

13

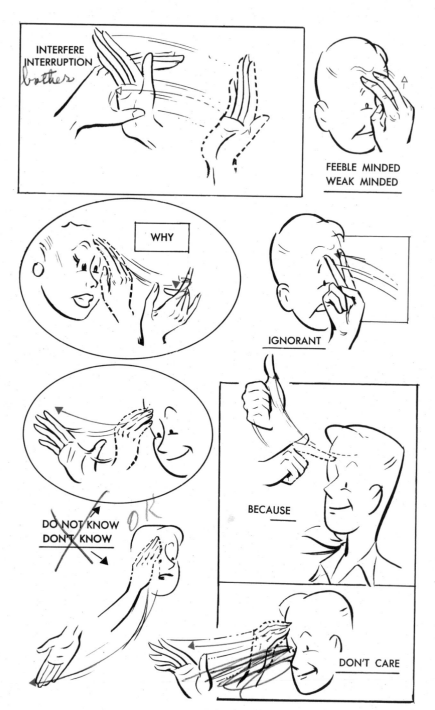

INTERFERE
INTERRUPTION
bother

FEEBLE MINDED
WEAK MINDED

WHY

IGNORANT

DO NOT KNOW
DON'T KNOW

BECAUSE

DON'T CARE

14

LIKE

As if the heart is being drawn out toward the object. The sign for "please" is also used to mean "like."

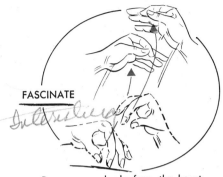

FASCINATE

Draw away slowly from the heart giving the face an intent or concentrated look.

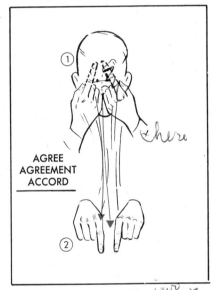

AGREE
AGREEMENT
ACCORD

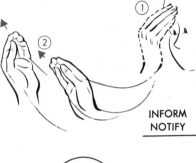

INFORM
NOTIFY

INTEND
MEAN
PURPOSE

SHOW
DISPLAY
DEMONSTRATE

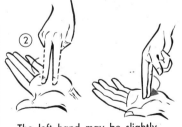

Push both hands forward or around as if exhibiting to some one.

The left hand may be slightly twisted around in an opposite way.

15

Cookies - Cake - Pie

(Made with one
or both hands.)

DENY
EVADE

INFLUENCE

ADVICE

(Made with one
or both hands.)

DON'T BELIEVE
DOUBT
Bend and unbend
fingers several
times.

CONFESS
ADMIT   (Get it off the chest)

SHOUT
YELL

BE QUIET
SILENCE

16

ANNOUNCE
MAKE KNOWN

To indicate something is PUBLISHED and announced in a newspaper, press hands palm upon palm and then proceed as above.

BLAME

To express the idea of ACCUSE extend both hands toward the person who is blamed.

To acknowledge oneself to blame, bring the sign toward you almost against the breast.

INNOCENCE is expressed by making the sign "blame" and "not".

FORGET
(SLIP THE MIND)

EXCUSE
FORGIVE

Move along the length of the hand and beyond.

REMEMBER
RECALL

PARDON

Rub back and forth on palm.

17

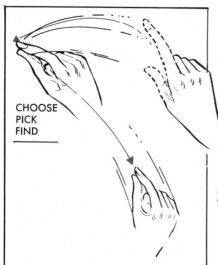

CHOOSE
PICK
FIND

~~PROPOSE~~
OFFER

As in the act of offering something to someone.

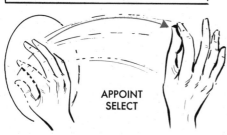

APPOINT
SELECT

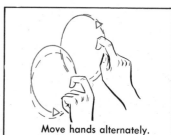

Move hands alternately.

EXAMINATION, QUIZ or **QUERY** (many questions)

paper

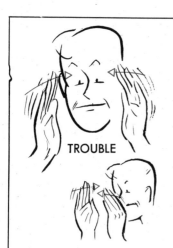

TROUBLE

WORRY
WORRIED

Move in circular motion alternately and look worried.

W Hand

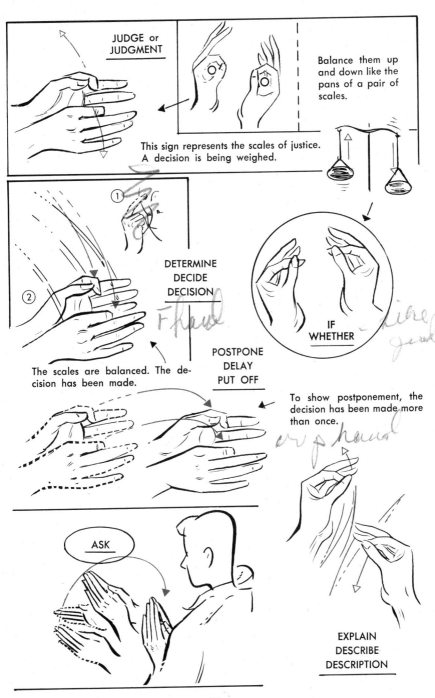

JUDGE or JUDGMENT

Balance them up and down like the pans of a pair of scales.

This sign represents the scales of justice. A decision is being weighed.

DETERMINE
DECIDE
DECISION

IF
WHETHER

The scales are balanced. The decision has been made.

POSTPONE
DELAY
PUT OFF

To show postponement, the decision has been made more than once.

ASK

EXPLAIN
DESCRIBE
DESCRIPTION

19

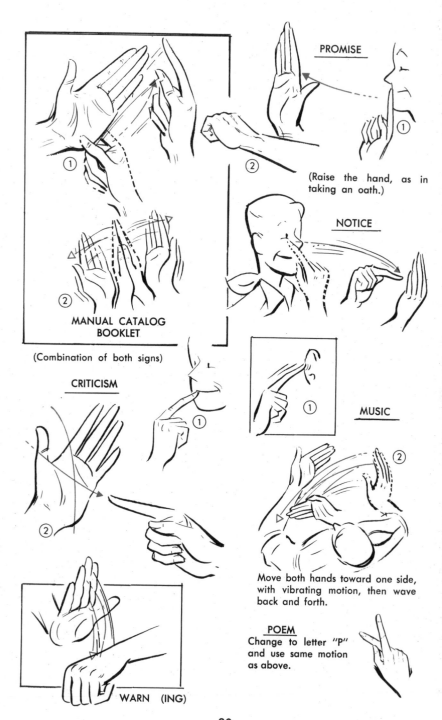

PROMISE

(Raise the hand, as in taking an oath.)

NOTICE

MANUAL CATALOG BOOKLET

(Combination of both signs)

CRITICISM

MUSIC

Move both hands toward one side, with vibrating motion, then wave back and forth.

POEM
Change to letter "P" and use same motion as above.

WARN (ING)

20

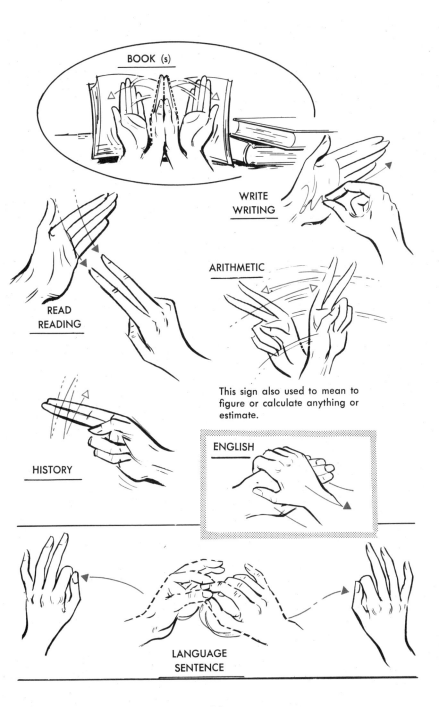

BOOK (s)

WRITE
WRITING

READ
READING

ARITHMETIC

This sign also used to mean to figure or calculate anything or estimate.

HISTORY

ENGLISH

LANGUAGE
SENTENCE

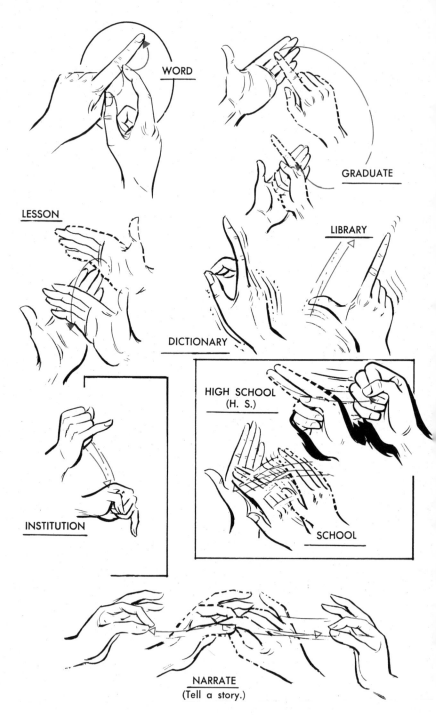

WORD

GRADUATE

LESSON

LIBRARY

DICTIONARY

HIGH SCHOOL
(H. S.)

INSTITUTION

SCHOOL

NARRATE
(Tell a story.)

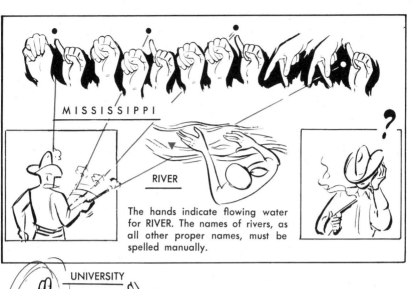

M I S S I S S I P P I

RIVER

The hands indicate flowing water for RIVER. The names of rivers, as all other proper names, must be spelled manually.

UNIVERSITY

The letter "U" made in a circling motion. The name of the university, of course, must be spelled.

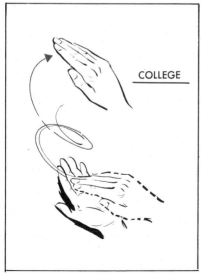

COLLEGE

GALLAUDET COLLEGE

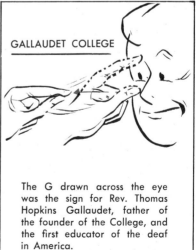

The G drawn across the eye was the sign for Rev. Thomas Hopkins Gallaudet, father of the founder of the College, and the first educator of the deaf in America.

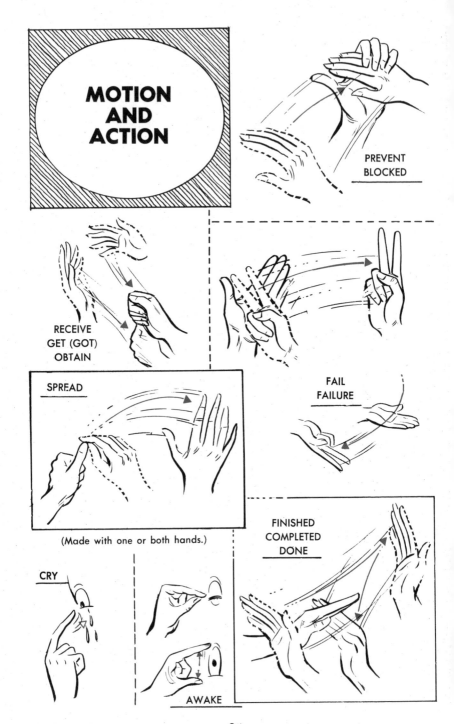

MOTION AND ACTION

PREVENT
BLOCKED

RECEIVE
GET (GOT)
OBTAIN

FAIL
FAILURE

SPREAD

(Made with one or both hands.)

FINISHED
COMPLETED
DONE

CRY

AWAKE

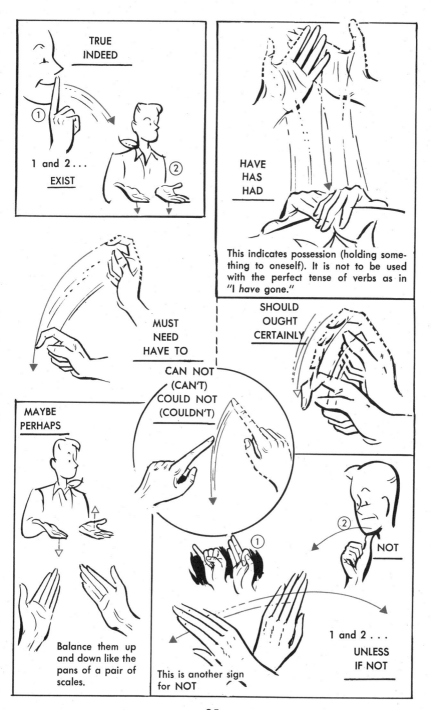

TRUE
INDEED

① 1 and 2...
EXIST ②

HAVE
HAS
HAD

This indicates possession (holding something to oneself). It is not to be used with the perfect tense of verbs as in "I *have* gone."

MUST
NEED
HAVE TO

SHOULD
OUGHT
CERTAINLY

CAN NOT
(CAN'T)
COULD NOT
(COULDN'T)

MAYBE
PERHAPS

① ②
NOT

Balance them up and down like the pans of a pair of scales.

This is another sign for NOT

1 and 2 . . .
UNLESS
IF NOT

25

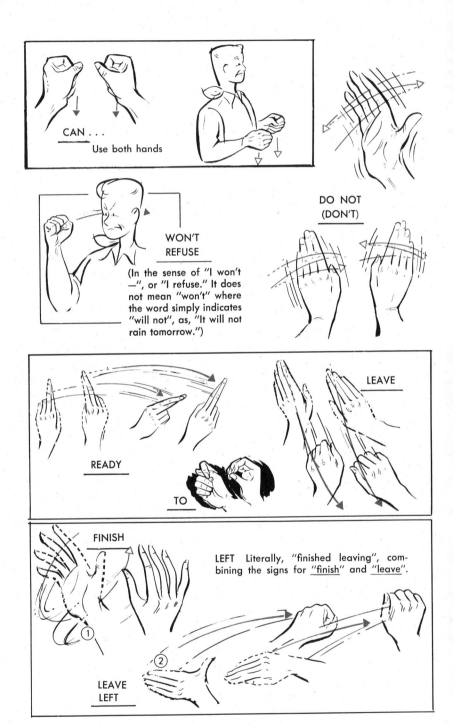

CAN . . .
Use both hands

DO NOT
(DON'T)

WON'T
REFUSE

(In the sense of "I won't —", or "I refuse." It does not mean "won't" where the word simply indicates "will not", as, "It will not rain tomorrow.")

READY

TO

LEAVE

FINISH

LEFT Literally, "finished leaving", combining the signs for "finish" and "leave".

LEAVE
LEFT

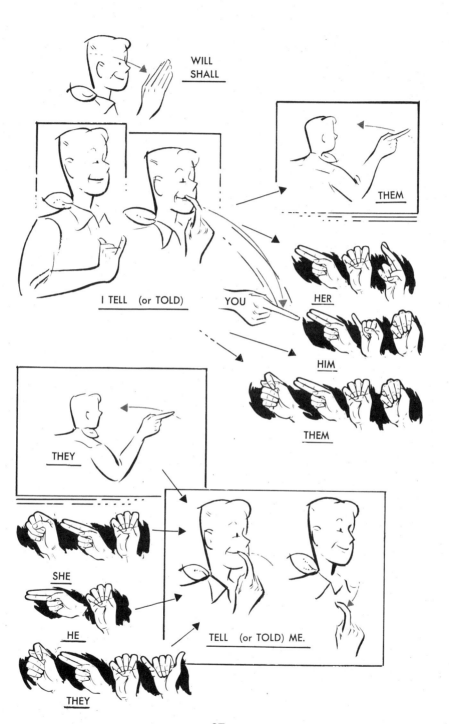

WILL
SHALL

THEM

I TELL (or TOLD)   YOU   HER

HIM

THEM

THEY

SHE

HE

THEY

TELL (or TOLD) ME.

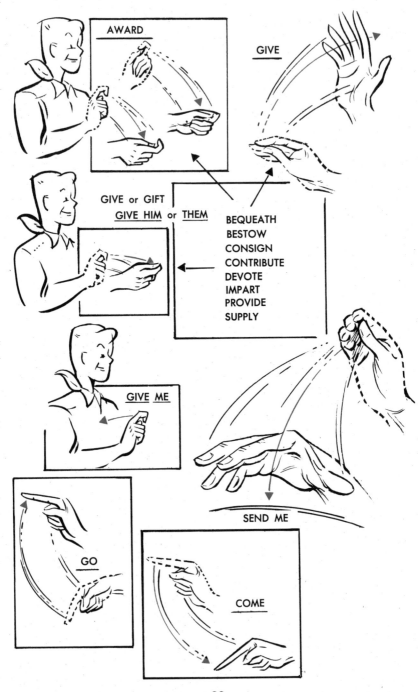

AWARD

GIVE

GIVE or GIFT
GIVE HIM or THEM

BEQUEATH
BESTOW
CONSIGN
CONTRIBUTE
DEVOTE
IMPART
PROVIDE
SUPPLY

GIVE ME

SEND ME

GO

COME

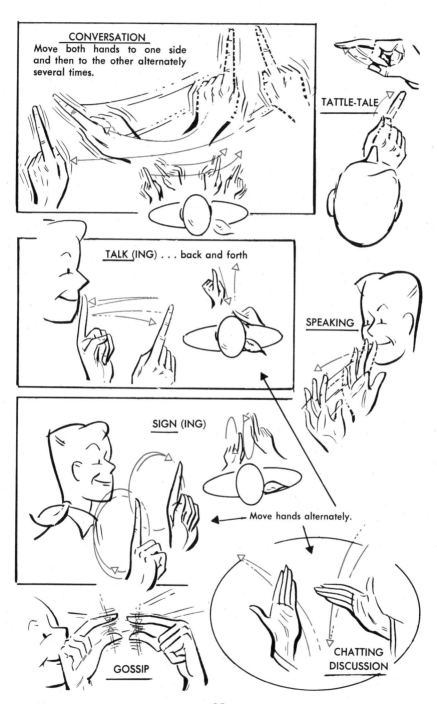

CONVERSATION
Move both hands to one side and then to the other alternately several times.

TATTLE-TALE

TALK (ING) . . . back and forth

SPEAKING

SIGN (ING)

Move hands alternately.

GOSSIP

CHATTING
DISCUSSION

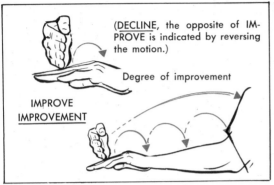

(DECLINE, the opposite of IM-PROVE is indicated by reversing the motion.)

Degree of improvement

IMPROVE
IMPROVEMENT

Quick

FAST

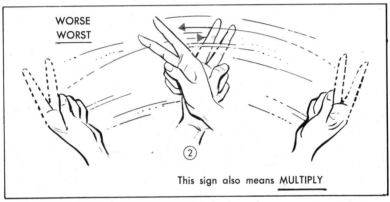

WORSE
WORST

②

This sign also means MULTIPLY

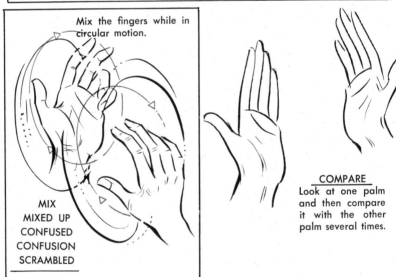

Mix the fingers while in circular motion.

MIX
MIXED UP
CONFUSED
CONFUSION
SCRAMBLED

COMPARE
Look at one palm and then compare it with the other palm several times.

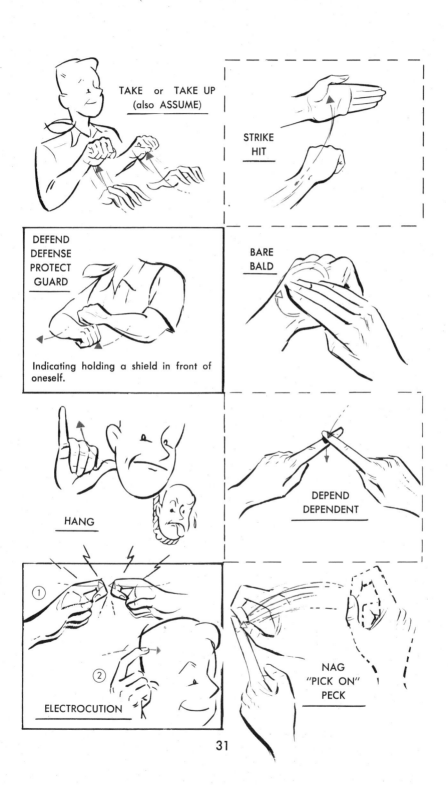

TAKE or TAKE UP
(also ASSUME)

STRIKE
HIT

DEFEND
DEFENSE
PROTECT
GUARD

Indicating holding a shield in front of
oneself.

BARE
BALD

HANG

DEPEND
DEPENDENT

ELECTROCUTION

NAG
"PICK ON"
PECK

ARRIVE (ING)

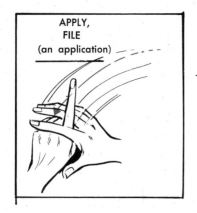

PASS, PASSING
As when one person passes another

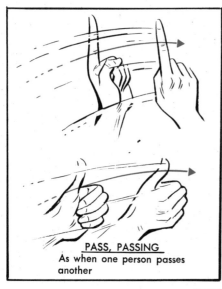

RACE
COMPETE

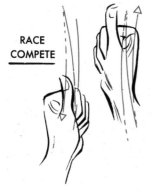

SHARE

APPLY,
FILE
(an application)

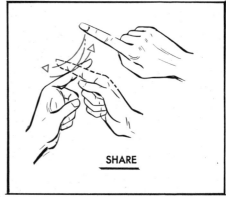

COME ALONE

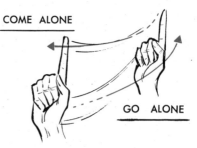

GO ALONE

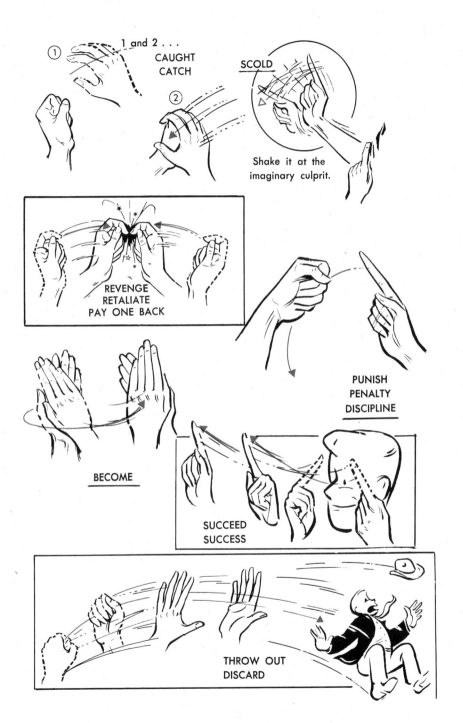

1 and 2 . . .
CAUGHT
CATCH

SCOLD

Shake it at the
imaginary culprit.

REVENGE
RETALIATE
PAY ONE BACK

PUNISH
PENALTY
DISCIPLINE

BECOME

SUCCEED
SUCCESS

THROW OUT
DISCARD

33

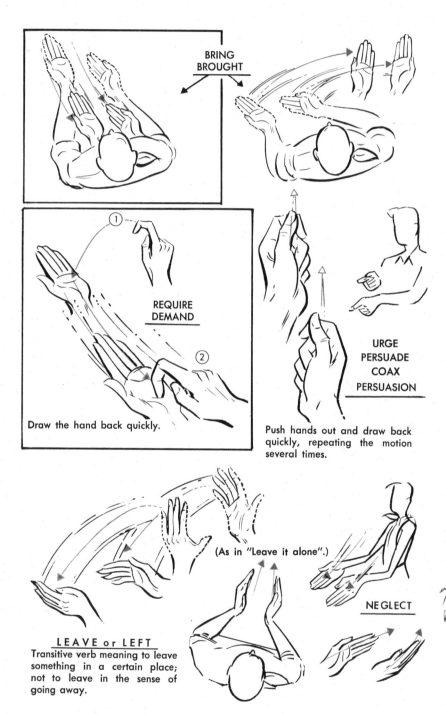

BRING
BROUGHT

REQUIRE
DEMAND

Draw the hand back quickly.

URGE
PERSUADE
COAX
PERSUASION

Push hands out and draw back
quickly, repeating the motion
several times.

(As in "Leave it alone".)

NEGLECT

LEAVE or LEFT
Transitive verb meaning to leave
something in a certain place;
not to leave in the sense of
going away.

34

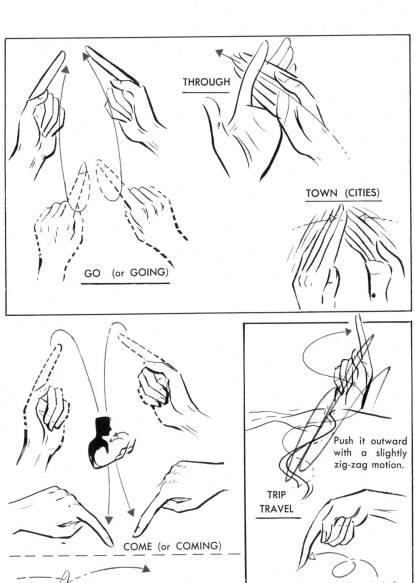

THROUGH

TOWN (CITIES)

GO (or GOING)

COME (or COMING)

GOING ON A

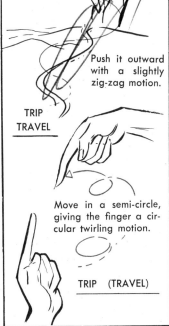

Push it outward with a slightly zig-zag motion.

TRIP TRAVEL

Move in a semi-circle, giving the finger a circular twirling motion.

TRIP (TRAVEL)

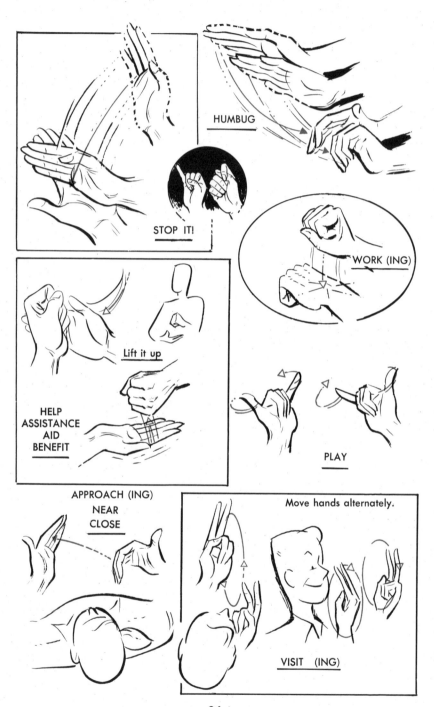

HUMBUG

STOP IT!

WORK (ING)

Lift it up

HELP
ASSISTANCE
AID
BENEFIT

PLAY

APPROACH (ING)
NEAR
CLOSE

Move hands alternately.

VISIT   (ING)

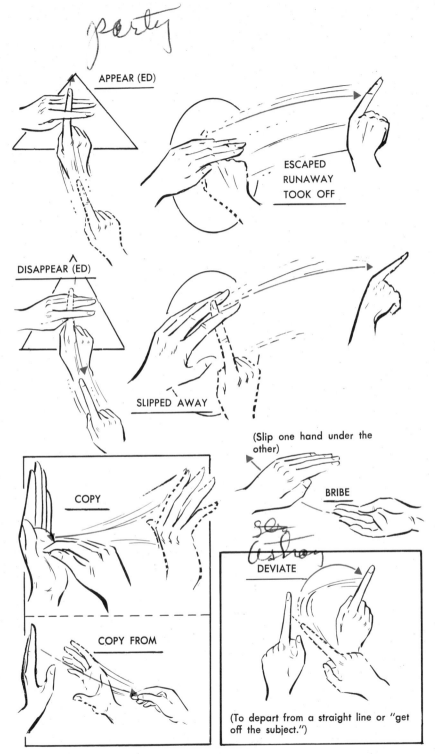

APPEAR (ED)

ESCAPED
RUNAWAY
TOOK OFF

DISAPPEAR (ED)

SLIPPED AWAY

(Slip one hand under the other)

COPY

BRIBE

COPY FROM

DEVIATE

(To depart from a straight line or "get off the subject.")

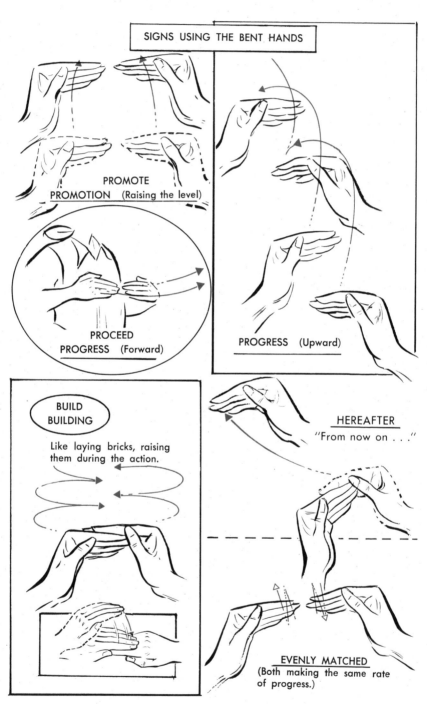

SIGNS USING THE BENT HANDS

PROMOTE
PROMOTION   (Raising the level)

PROCEED
PROGRESS   (Forward)

PROGRESS   (Upward)

BUILD
BUILDING

Like laying bricks, raising
them during the action.

HEREAFTER
"From now on . . ."

EVENLY MATCHED
(Both making the same rate
of progress.)

even

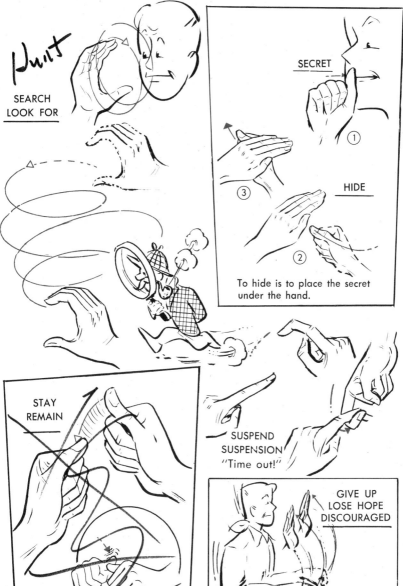

Meat + Overcome — I fish[?]

Hurt

SEARCH
LOOK FOR

SECRET

①

③

HIDE

②

To hide is to place the secret
under the hand.

STAY
REMAIN

SUSPEND
SUSPENSION
"Time out!"

GIVE UP
LOSE HOPE
DISCOURAGED

Simultaneously with the action
draw the head and shoulders
back somewhat.

Remain

Push 1 thumb
with either away

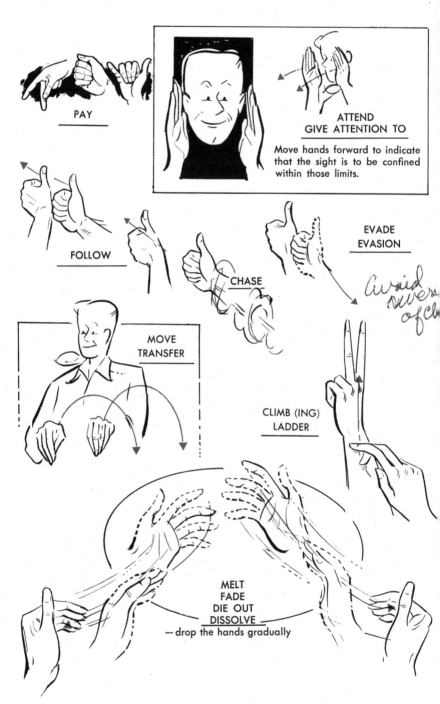

PAY

ATTEND
GIVE ATTENTION TO

Move hands forward to indicate that the sight is to be confined within those limits.

FOLLOW

CHASE

EVADE
EVASION

MOVE
TRANSFER

CLIMB (ING)
LADDER

MELT
FADE
DIE OUT
DISSOLVE
— drop the hands gradually

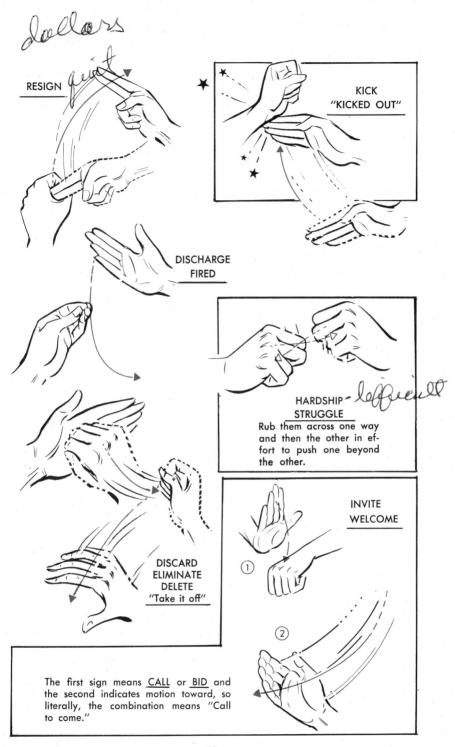

RESIGN

KICK
"KICKED OUT"

DISCHARGE
FIRED

HARDSHIP
STRUGGLE
Rub them across one way
and then the other in ef-
fort to push one beyond
the other.

INVITE
WELCOME

①

②

DISCARD
ELIMINATE
DELETE
"Take it off"

The first sign means <u>CALL</u> or <u>BID</u> and
the second indicates motion toward, so
literally, the combination means "Call
to come."

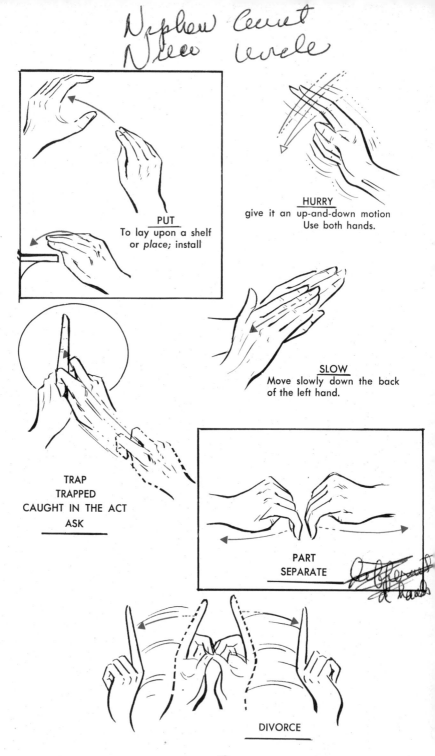

Nephew Count
Niece circle

PUT
To lay upon a shelf
or *place;* install

HURRY
give it an up-and-down motion
Use both hands.

SLOW
Move slowly down the back
of the left hand.

TRAP
TRAPPED
CAUGHT IN THE ACT
ASK

PART
SEPARATE

DIVORCE

42

Kind - Hand ceiling waist hi - Sincere

SENSATIONS
FEELINGS
AND
AFFECTIONS

LOVE
Press over the heart

LAUGH
SMILE

①

1 and 2 . . .
CHEERFUL

② Move fingers rapidly to indicate the "beams of joy" radiating from the face and look as cheerful as you can.

HYSTERICAL LAUGH

(Rolling all over the aisle)

CONSCIENCE

THUMP!

THUMP!

JEALOUS
ENVY

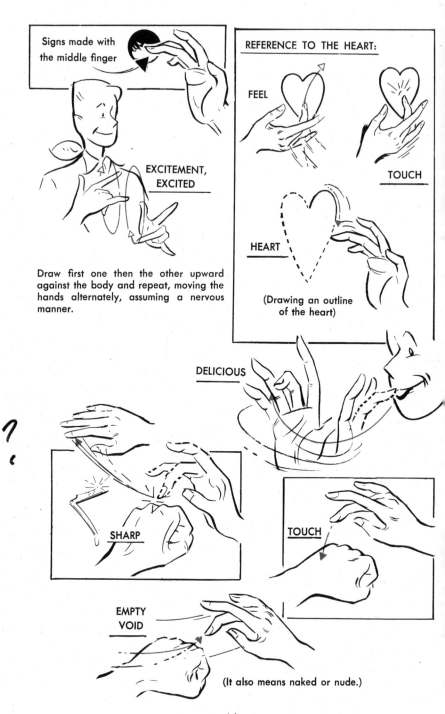

Signs made with the middle finger

EXCITEMENT, EXCITED

Draw first one then the other upward against the body and repeat, moving the hands alternately, assuming a nervous manner.

REFERENCE TO THE HEART:

FEEL

TOUCH

HEART

(Drawing an outline of the heart)

DELICIOUS

SHARP

TOUCH

EMPTY VOID

(It also means naked or nude.)

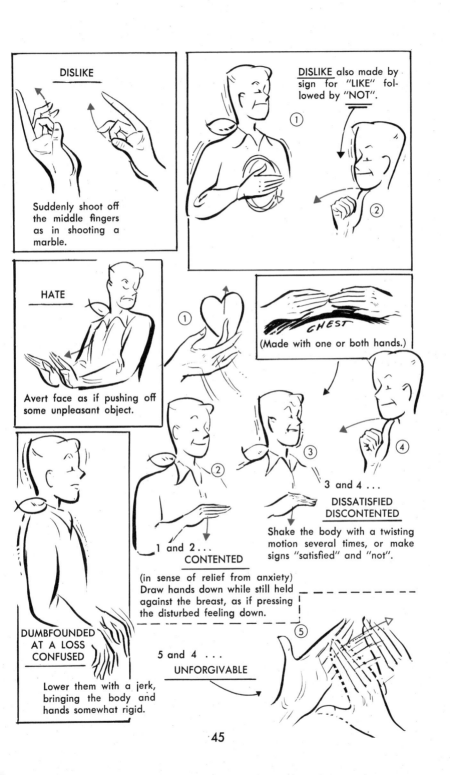

DISLIKE

Suddenly shoot off the middle fingers as in shooting a marble.

DISLIKE also made by sign for "LIKE" followed by "NOT".

HATE

Avert face as if pushing off some unpleasant object.

(Made with one or both hands.)

1 and 2 . . .
CONTENTED

(in sense of relief from anxiety) Draw hands down while still held against the breast, as if pressing the disturbed feeling down.

3 and 4 . . .
DISSATISFIED DISCONTENTED

Shake the body with a twisting motion several times, or make signs "satisfied" and "not".

DUMBFOUNDED AT A LOSS CONFUSED

Lower them with a jerk, bringing the body and hands somewhat rigid.

5 and 4 . . .
UNFORGIVABLE

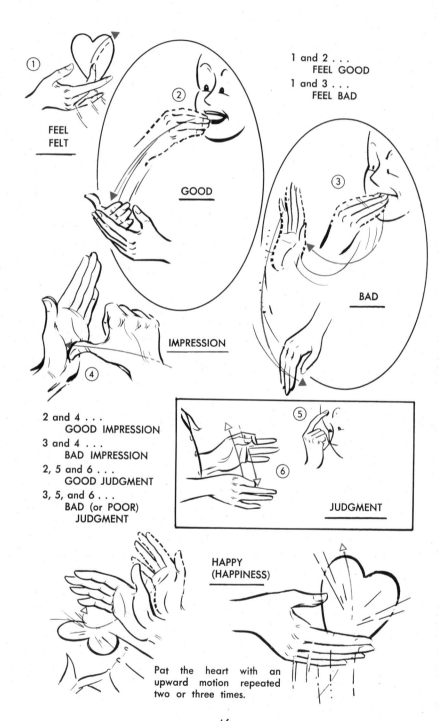

① FEEL
FELT

② GOOD

③ BAD

1 and 2 . . .
    FEEL GOOD
1 and 3 . . .
    FEEL BAD

④ IMPRESSION

2 and 4 . . .
    GOOD IMPRESSION
3 and 4 . . .
    BAD IMPRESSION
2, 5 and 6 . . .
    GOOD JUDGMENT
3, 5, and 6 . . .
    BAD (or POOR)
    JUDGMENT

⑤ ⑥ JUDGMENT

HAPPY
(HAPPINESS)

Pat the heart with an upward motion repeated two or three times.

46

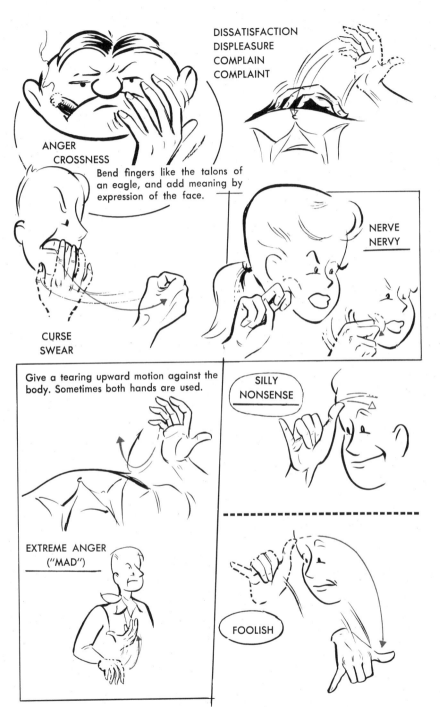

ANGER
CROSSNESS

DISSATISFACTION
DISPLEASURE
COMPLAIN
COMPLAINT

Bend fingers like the talons of an eagle, and add meaning by expression of the face.

NERVE
NERVY

CURSE
SWEAR

Give a tearing upward motion against the body. Sometimes both hands are used.

SILLY
NONSENSE

EXTREME ANGER
("MAD")

FOOLISH

47

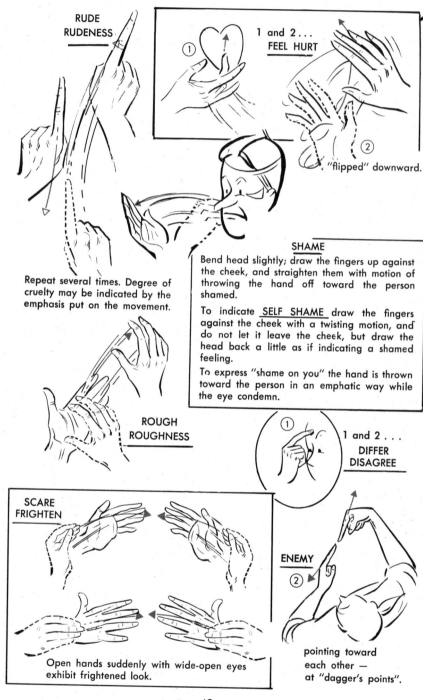

RUDE
RUDENESS

1 and 2...
FEEL HURT

"flipped" downward.

Repeat several times. Degree of cruelty may be indicated by the emphasis put on the movement.

SHAME

Bend head slightly; draw the fingers up against the cheek, and straighten them with motion of throwing the hand off toward the person shamed.

To indicate **SELF SHAME** draw the fingers against the cheek with a twisting motion, and do not let it leave the cheek, but draw the head back a little as if indicating a shamed feeling.

To express "shame on you" the hand is thrown toward the person in an emphatic way while the eye condemn.

ROUGH
ROUGHNESS

1 and 2 . . .
DIFFER
DISAGREE

SCARE
FRIGHTEN

ENEMY

Open hands suddenly with wide-open eyes exhibit frightened look.

pointing toward each other — at "dagger's points".

48

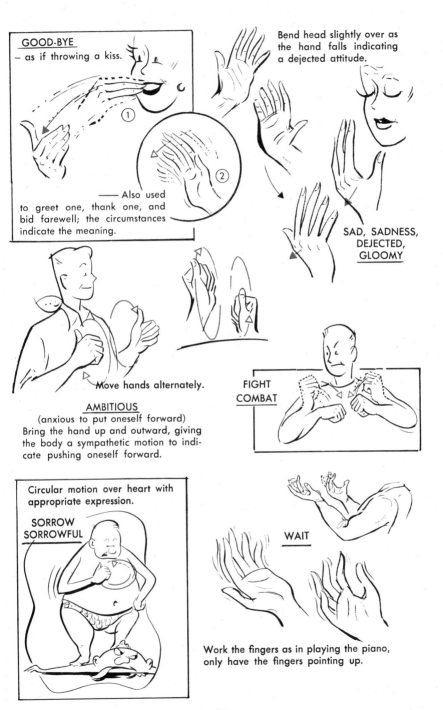

GOOD-BYE
— as if throwing a kiss.

①

② —— Also used to greet one, thank one, and bid farewell; the circumstances indicate the meaning.

Bend head slightly over as the hand falls indicating a dejected attitude.

SAD, SADNESS, DEJECTED, GLOOMY

Move hands alternately.

AMBITIOUS
(anxious to put oneself forward)
Bring the hand up and outward, giving the body a sympathetic motion to indicate pushing oneself forward.

FIGHT COMBAT

Circular motion over heart with appropriate expression.

SORROW SORROWFUL

WAIT

Work the fingers as in playing the piano, only have the fingers pointing up.

49

WONDER
ASTONISHMENT

Throw hands up in amazement.

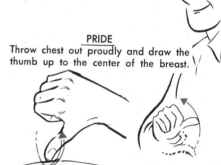

PRIDE
Throw chest out proudly and draw the thumb up to the center of the breast.

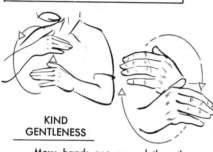

KIND
GENTLENESS

Move hands one around the other in a circle.

BRAG (GING)
BOAST (ING)

FUNNY
HUMOROUS
Two or three times and look funny.

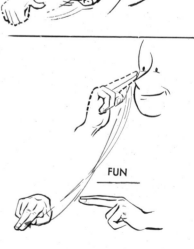

FUN

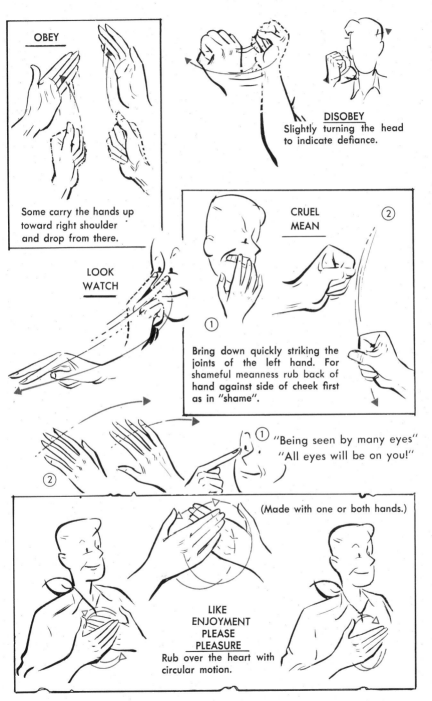

OBEY

Some carry the hands up toward right shoulder and drop from there.

DISOBEY
Slightly turning the head to indicate defiance.

LOOK WATCH

CRUEL MEAN

Bring down quickly striking the joints of the left hand. For shameful meanness rub back of hand against side of cheek first as in "shame".

"Being seen by many eyes"
"All eyes will be on you!"

(Made with one or both hands.)

**LIKE
ENJOYMENT
PLEASE
PLEASURE**
Rub over the heart with circular motion.

51

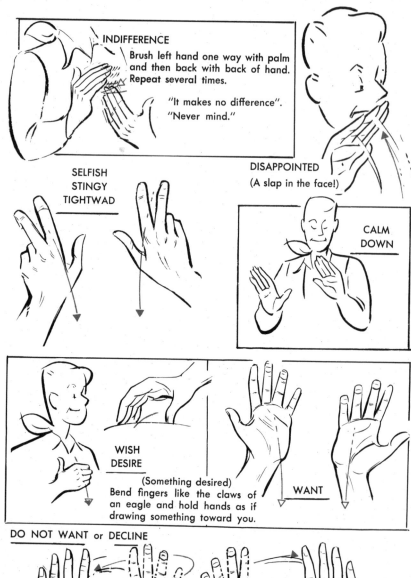

INDIFFERENCE

Brush left hand one way with palm and then back with back of hand. Repeat several times.

"It makes no difference".
"Never mind."

DISAPPOINTED
(A slap in the face!)

SELFISH
STINGY
TIGHTWAD

CALM
DOWN

WISH
DESIRE

(Something desired)
Bend fingers like the claws of an eagle and hold hands as if drawing something toward you.

WANT

DO NOT WANT or DECLINE

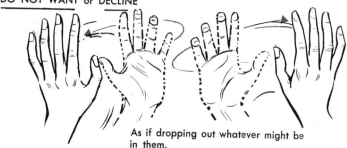

As if dropping out whatever might be in them.

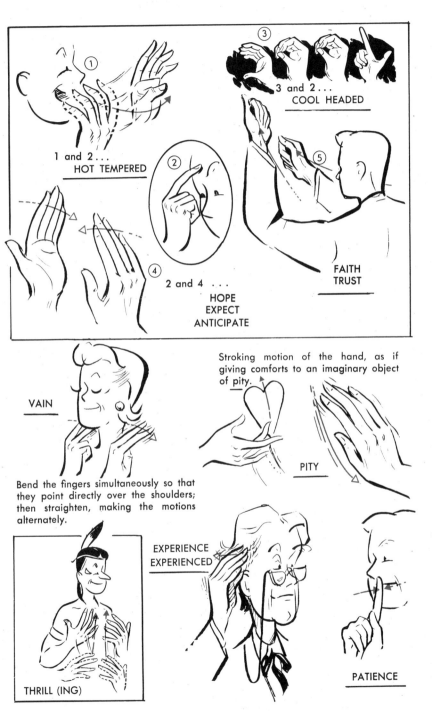

1 and 2...
HOT TEMPERED

2
4   2 and 4 ...
HOPE
EXPECT
ANTICIPATE

3   3 and 2...
COOL HEADED

5   FAITH
TRUST

VAIN

Bend the fingers simultaneously so that they point directly over the shoulders; then straighten, making the motions alternately.

Stroking motion of the hand, as if giving comforts to an imaginary object of pity.

PITY

EXPERIENCE
EXPERIENCED

THRILL (ING)

PATIENCE

53

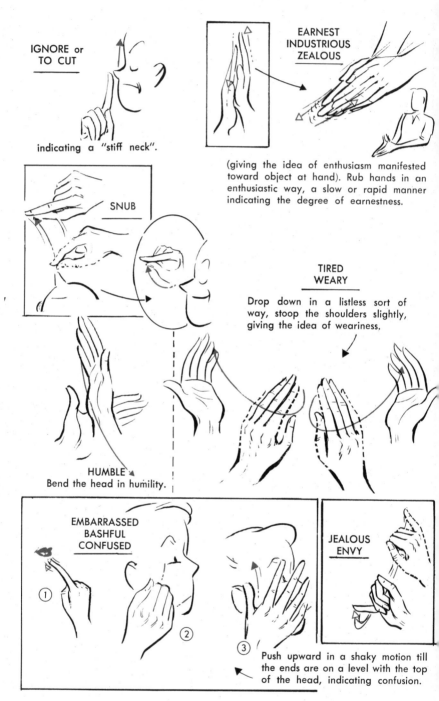

IGNORE or
TO CUT

indicating a "stiff neck".

EARNEST
INDUSTRIOUS
ZEALOUS

(giving the idea of enthusiasm manifested toward object at hand). Rub hands in an enthusiastic way, a slow or rapid manner indicating the degree of earnestness.

SNUB

TIRED
WEARY

Drop down in a listless sort of way, stoop the shoulders slightly, giving the idea of weariness.

HUMBLE
Bend the head in humility.

EMBARRASSED
BASHFUL
CONFUSED

①

②

③

JEALOUS
ENVY

Push upward in a shaky motion till the ends are on a level with the top of the head, indicating confusion.

54

HEARING
HEARD

— as if listening

SEE

(Idea of vision). Ends of fingers representing direction of light.

TALK
VERBAL
SPEAK
SPEECH
SAY

NOTHING

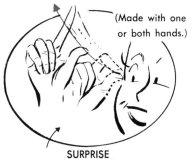

(Made with one or both hands.)

SURPRISE
Representing the motion of opening the eyes suddenly and look surprise.

PATIENCE
PATIENT

Press on lips and bow head in resignation; repeat latter motion once or twice.

TEDIOUS
MONOTONOUS ("The Grind".)

TEDIOUS
Bend head forward slightly as if in obedience to the pressure of the finger.

ADJECTIVES

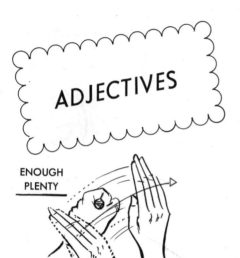

**ENOUGH
PLENTY**

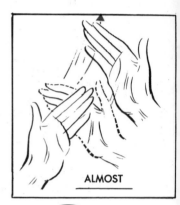

ALMOST

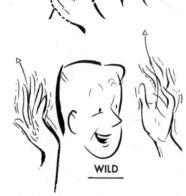

WILD

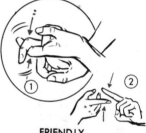

**FRIENDLY
FRIENDSHIP**
Clasp one above the other. Then bring them apart and clasp again but in opposite direction.

SMOOTH
Rub the end of the thumb against the ends of the fingers drawing the hands away from each other. The sign also indicates "of fine quality".

**HIGH
PROMINENT**

**BASE
LOW**

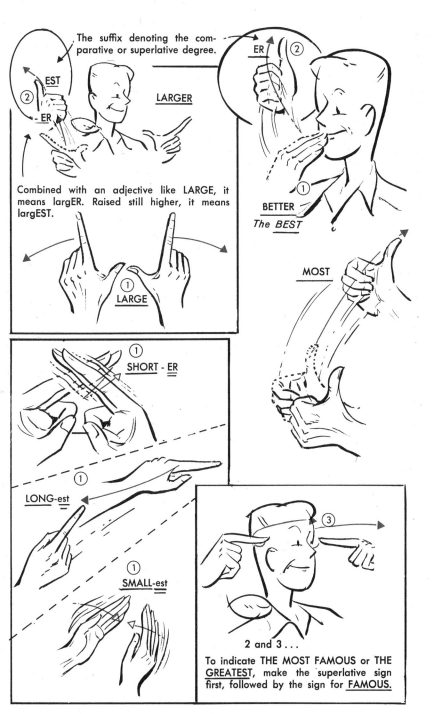

The suffix denoting the comparative or superlative degree.

EST
②
- ER

LARGER

ER
②

Combined with an adjective like LARGE, it means largER. Raised still higher, it means largEST.

BETTER
The BEST

① LARGE

MOST

① SHORT - ER

① LONG-est

① SMALL-est

2 and 3...
To indicate THE MOST FAMOUS or THE GREATEST, make the superlative sign first, followed by the sign for FAMOUS.

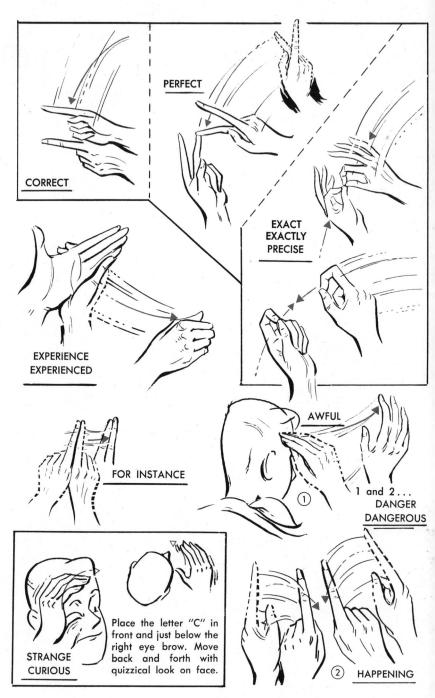

CORRECT

PERFECT

EXACT
EXACTLY
PRECISE

EXPERIENCE
EXPERIENCED

FOR INSTANCE

AWFUL

1 and 2...
DANGER
DANGEROUS

①

STRANGE
CURIOUS

Place the letter "C" in front and just below the right eye brow. Move back and forth with quizzical look on face.

② HAPPENING

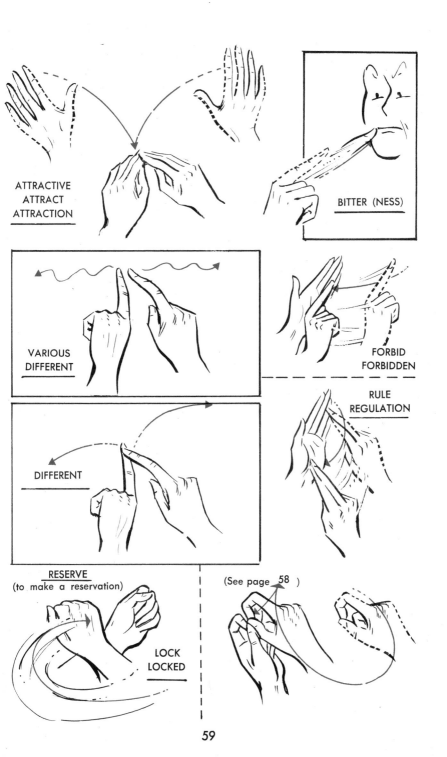

ATTRACTIVE
ATTRACT
ATTRACTION

BITTER (NESS)

VARIOUS
DIFFERENT

FORBID
FORBIDDEN

RULE
REGULATION

DIFFERENT

RESERVE
(to make a reservation)

LOCK
LOCKED

(See page 58)

59

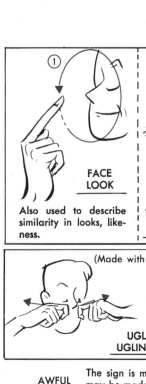

FACE
LOOK

Also used to describe similarity in looks, likeness.

1 and 2... ②
HANDSOME

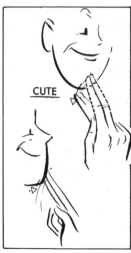

CUTE

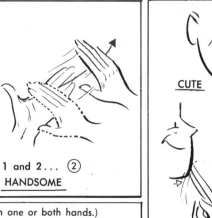

(Made with one or both hands.)

UGLY
UGLINESS

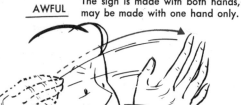

AWFUL

The sign is made with both hands, or may be made with one hand only.

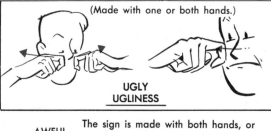

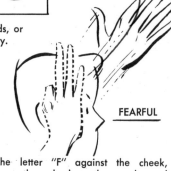

FEARFUL

The letter "F" against the cheek, move them slowly to the temples and finish as above in "awful".

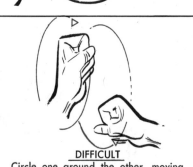

DIFFICULT

Circle one around the other, moving both at the same time. Make a show of some effort in moving the hands.

TOUGH
HARDBOILED

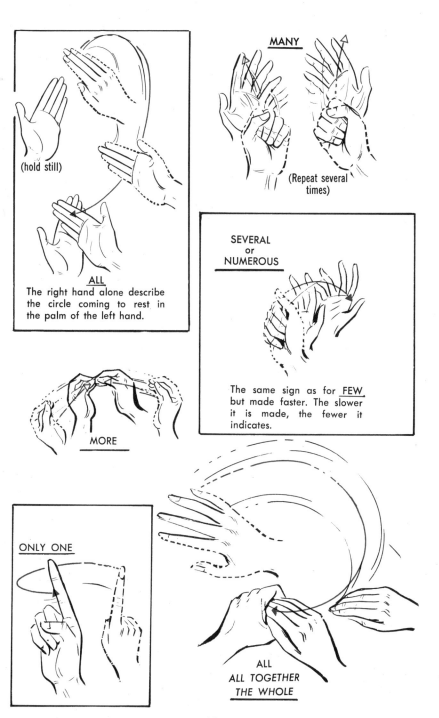

MANY

(Repeat several times)

(hold still)

ALL

The right hand alone describe the circle coming to rest in the palm of the left hand.

SEVERAL
or
NUMEROUS

The same sign as for FEW but made faster. The slower it is made, the fewer it indicates.

MORE

ONLY ONE

ALL
ALL TOGETHER
THE WHOLE

TRUE,
TRUTH,
REAL,
REALLY

DRY,
DULL,
BORING

Oh!

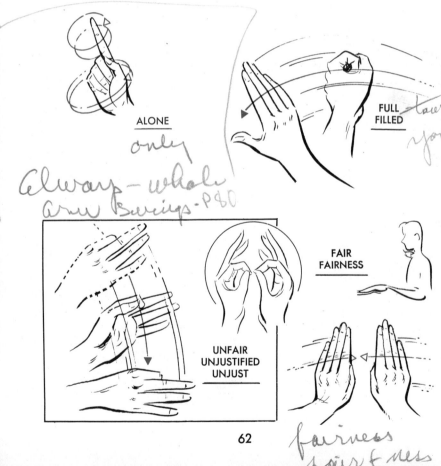

ALONE

FULL
FILLED

only

Always — whole
Arm Swings - P80

FAIR
FAIRNESS

UNFAIR
UNJUSTIFIED
UNJUST

fairness
fair f ness

Move hands simultaneously

**DIRTY
FILTH
FILTHY**

**ACTION
ACTIVE**

CLEANING
Move hand back and forth rapidly.

**IDLE
FREE
LEISURE
VACATION**

**CLEAN
PURE**

Move hand slowly once and with
slight pressure on **palm**.

NEAT

POLISH (ED)

GLISTEN (ING)

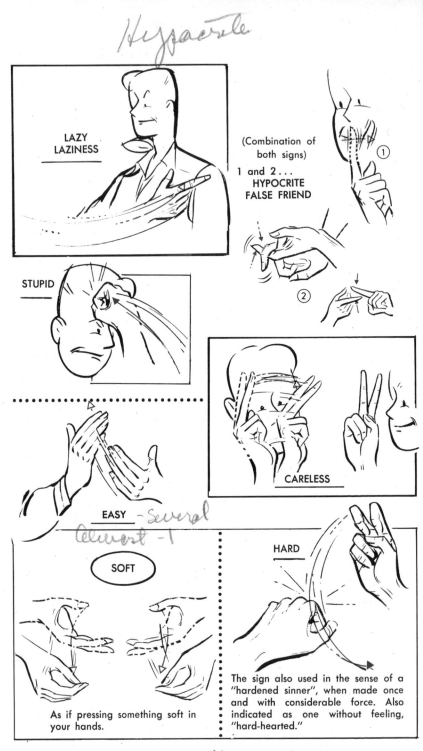

Hypocrite

LAZY
LAZINESS

(Combination of both signs)

1 and 2 . . .
HYPOCRITE
FALSE FRIEND

①

②

STUPID

CARELESS

EASY — Several
almost — 1

SOFT

HARD

As if pressing something soft in your hands.

The sign also used in the sense of a "hardened sinner", when made once and with considerable force. Also indicated as one without feeling, "hard-hearted."

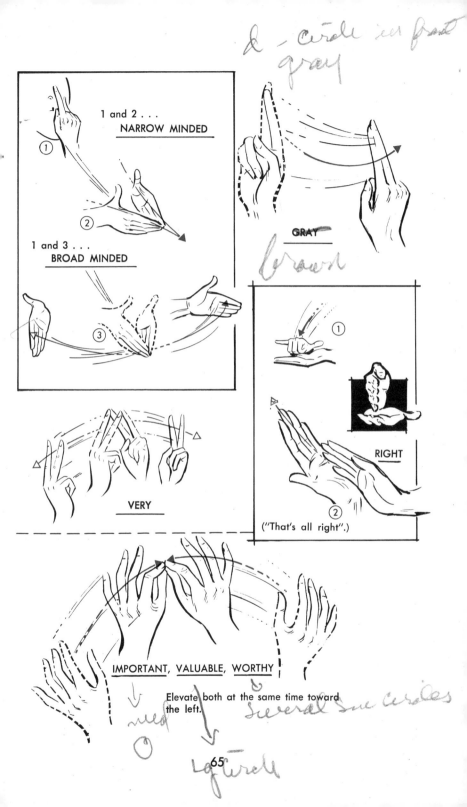

1 and 2 . . .
NARROW MINDED

1 and 3 . . .
BROAD MINDED

GRAY

VERY

RIGHT

("That's all right".)

IMPORTANT, VALUABLE, WORTHY

Elevate both at the same time toward the left.

65

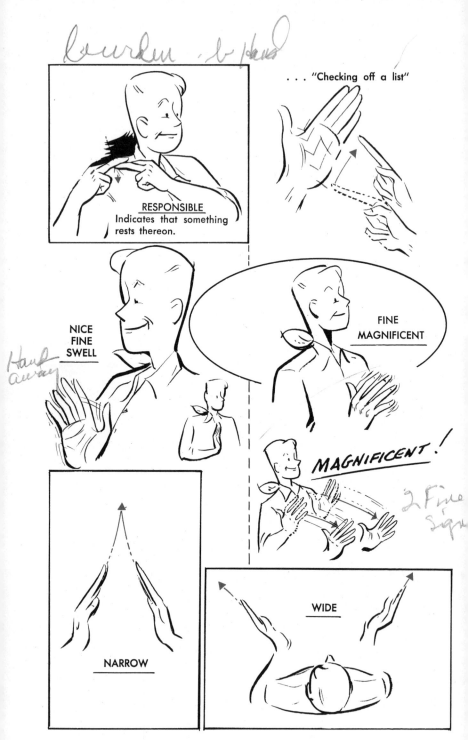

... "Checking off a list"

RESPONSIBLE
Indicates that something rests thereon.

NICE
FINE
SWELL

FINE
MAGNIFICENT

MAGNIFICENT !

NARROW

WIDE

66

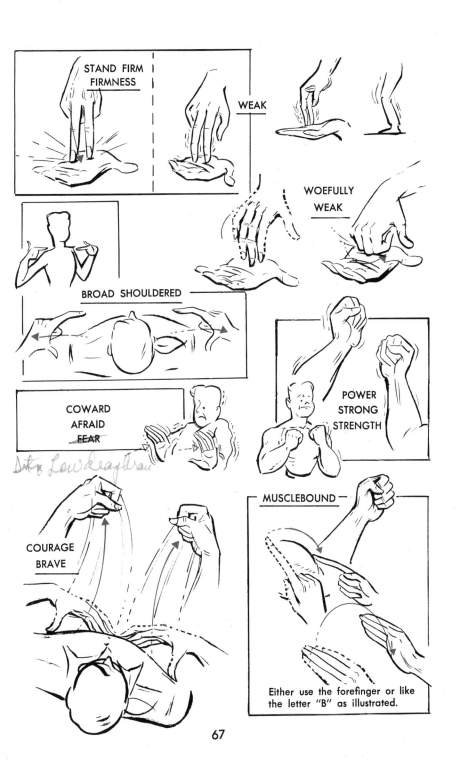

STAND FIRM
FIRMNESS

WEAK

WOEFULLY
WEAK

BROAD SHOULDERED

COWARD
AFRAID
FEAR

POWER
STRONG
STRENGTH

COURAGE
BRAVE

MUSCLEBOUND

Either use the forefinger or like
the letter "B" as illustrated.

67

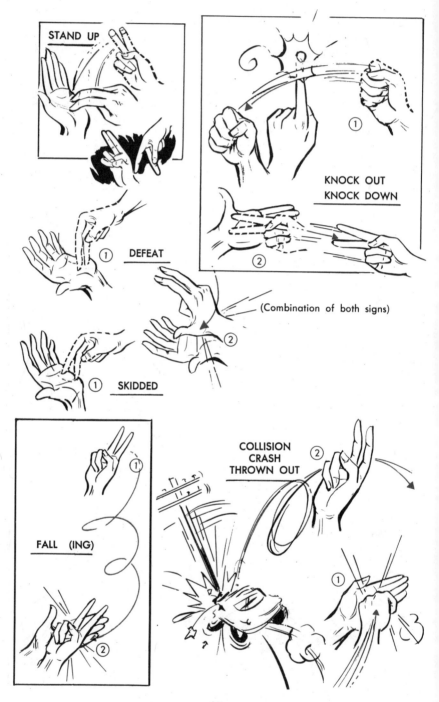

STAND UP

KNOCK OUT
KNOCK DOWN

① DEFEAT

②

(Combination of both signs)

① SKIDDED

FALL (ING)

COLLISION
CRASH
THROWN OUT

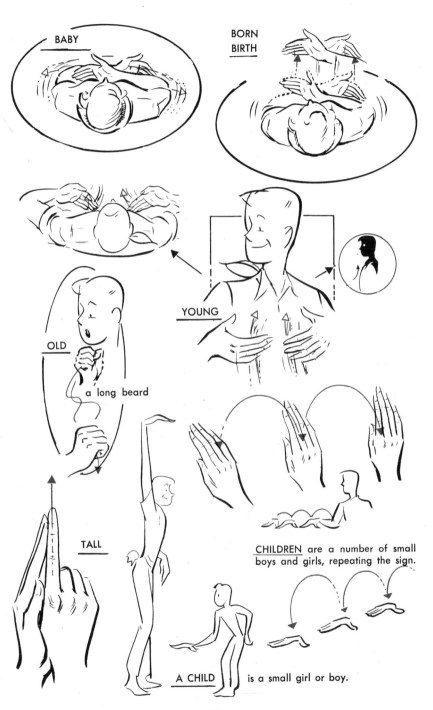

BABY

BORN
BIRTH

YOUNG

OLD

a long beard

TALL

CHILDREN are a number of small
boys and girls, repeating the sign.

A CHILD is a small girl or boy.

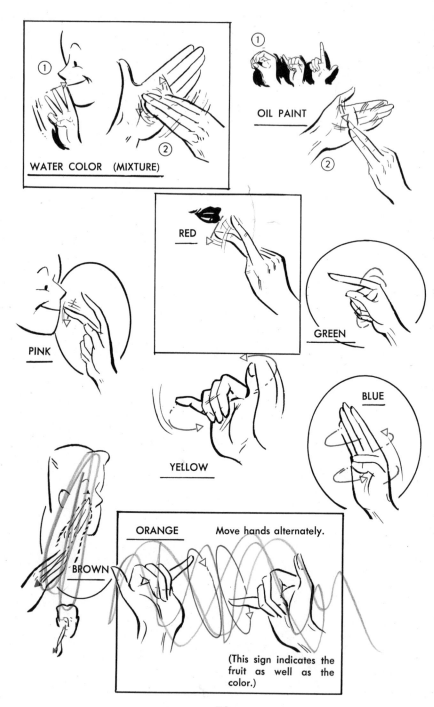

WATER COLOR (MIXTURE)

OIL PAINT

RED

PINK

GREEN

BLUE

YELLOW

ORANGE Move hands alternately.

BROWN

(This sign indicates the fruit as well as the color.)

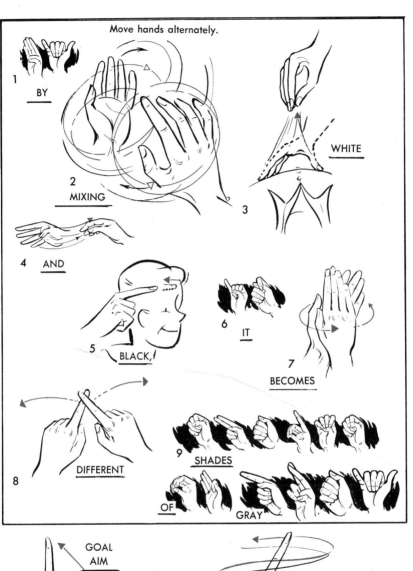

Move hands alternately.

1 BY

2 MIXING

3 WHITE

4 AND

5 BLACK,

6 IT

7 BECOMES

8 DIFFERENT

9 SHADES

OF

GRAY

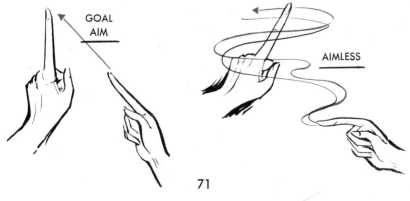

GOAL
AIM

AIMLESS

71

Time

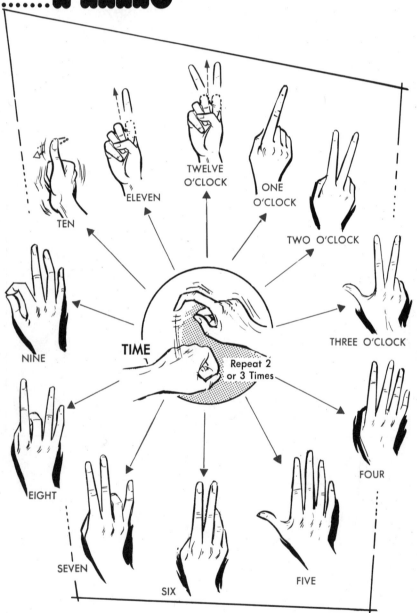

TEN

ELEVEN

TWELVE O'CLOCK

ONE O'CLOCK

TWO O'CLOCK

THREE O'CLOCK

NINE

TIME

Repeat 2 or 3 Times

FOUR

EIGHT

SEVEN

SIX

FIVE

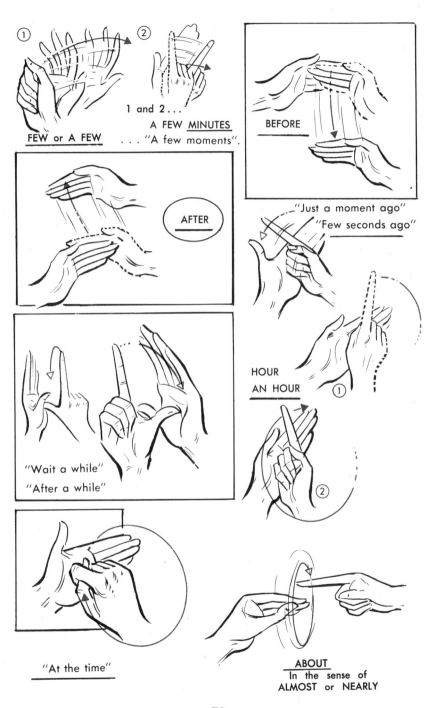

① ②

1 and 2...
A FEW <u>MINUTES</u>
... "A few moments".

<u>FEW or A FEW</u>

BEFORE

AFTER

"Just a moment ago"
"Few seconds ago"

HOUR
<u>AN HOUR</u>
①
②

"Wait a while"
"After a while"

"At the time"

<u>ABOUT</u>
In the sense of
ALMOST or NEARLY

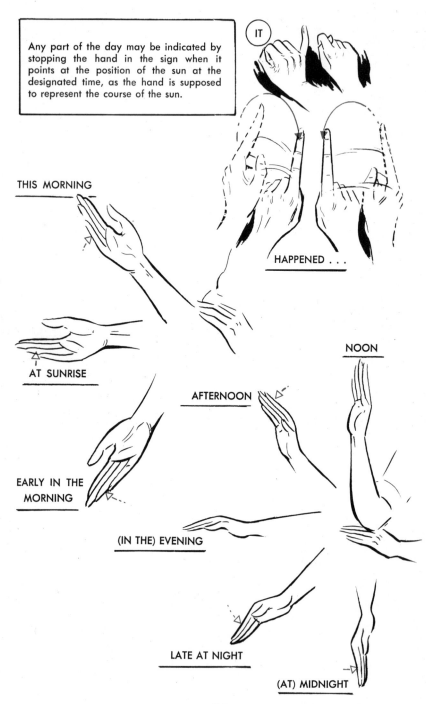

Any part of the day may be indicated by stopping the hand in the sign when it points at the position of the sun at the designated time, as the hand is supposed to represent the course of the sun.

IT

HAPPENED . . .

THIS MORNING

AT SUNRISE

NOON

AFTERNOON

EARLY IN THE MORNING

(IN THE) EVENING

LATE AT NIGHT

(AT) MIDNIGHT

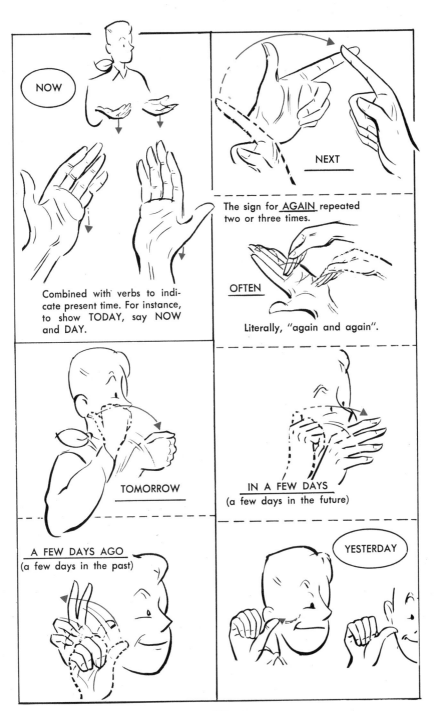

NOW

Combined with verbs to indicate present time. For instance, to show TODAY, say NOW and DAY.

NEXT

The sign for AGAIN repeated two or three times.

OFTEN

Literally, "again and again".

TOMORROW

IN A FEW DAYS
(a few days in the future)

A FEW DAYS AGO
(a few days in the past)

YESTERDAY

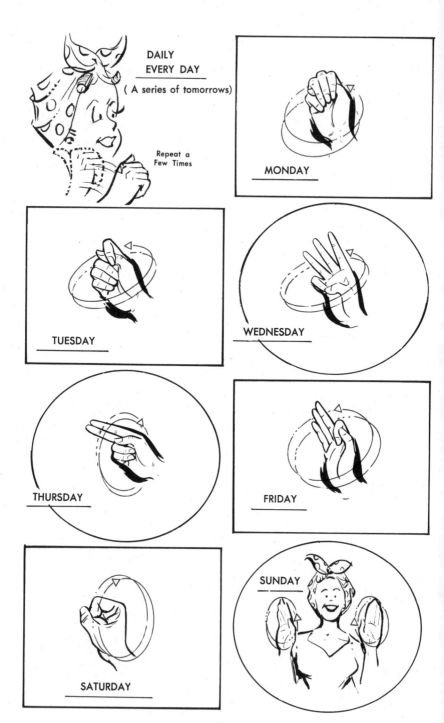

DAILY
EVERY DAY

(A series of tomorrows)

Repeat a
Few Times

MONDAY

TUESDAY

WEDNESDAY

THURSDAY

FRIDAY

SATURDAY

SUNDAY

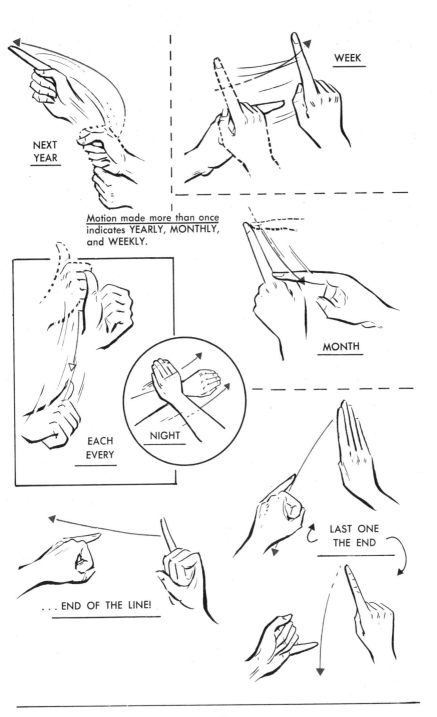

NEXT
YEAR

WEEK

Motion made more than once
indicates YEARLY, MONTHLY,
and WEEKLY.

MONTH

EACH
EVERY

NIGHT

LAST ONE
THE END

... END OF THE LINE!

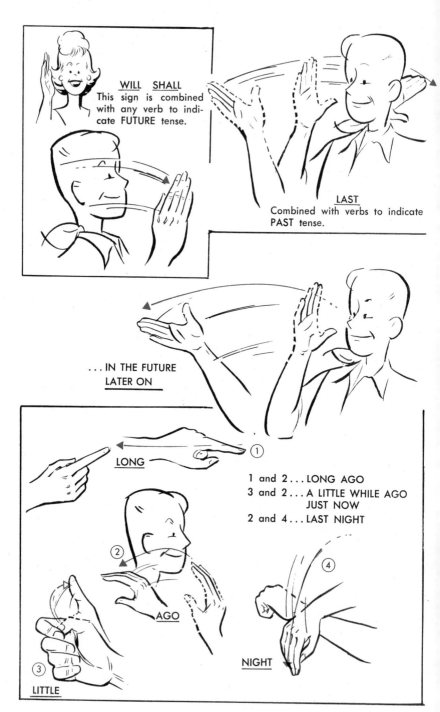

WILL   SHALL
This sign is combined with any verb to indicate FUTURE tense.

LAST
Combined with verbs to indicate PAST tense.

... IN THE FUTURE
LATER ON

LONG

1 and 2 ... LONG AGO
3 and 2 ... A LITTLE WHILE AGO
              JUST NOW
2 and 4 ... LAST NIGHT

AGO

NIGHT

LITTLE

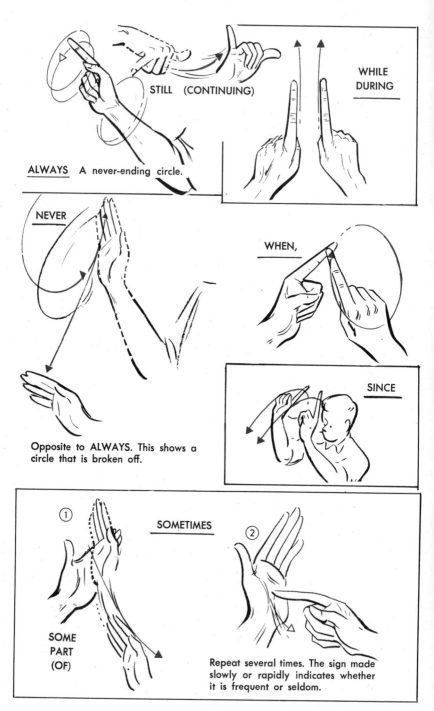

STILL (CONTINUING)

WHILE
DURING

ALWAYS A never-ending circle.

NEVER

WHEN,

SINCE

Opposite to ALWAYS. This shows a
circle that is broken off.

SOMETIMES

① ②

SOME
PART
(OF)

Repeat several times. The sign made
slowly or rapidly indicates whether
it is frequent or seldom.

Numbers & Counting

2 + 2 =

FOR NUMBERS 1 TO 12
See page 72

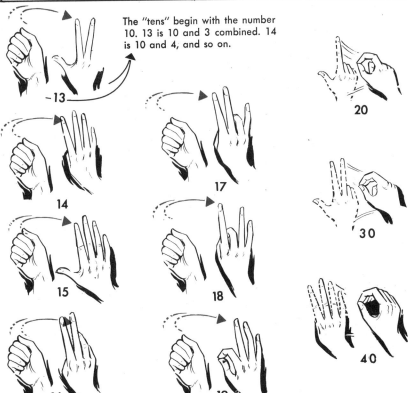

The "tens" begin with the number 10. 13 is 10 and 3 combined. 14 is 10 and 4, and so on.

13

14

15

16

17

18

19

20

30

40

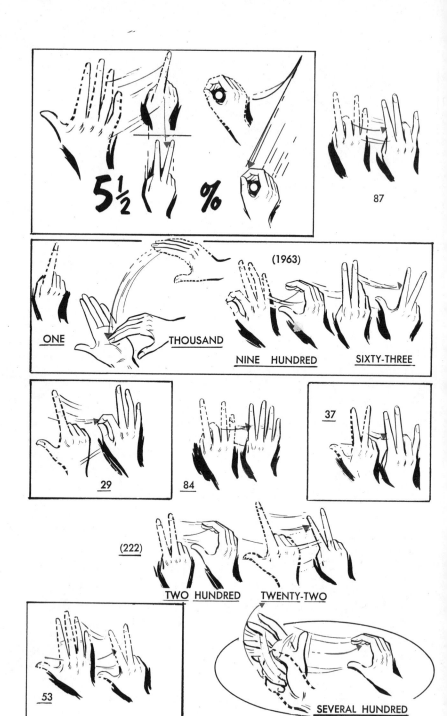

5½ % 87

(1963)

ONE THOUSAND NINE HUNDRED SIXTY-THREE

29 84 37

(222)

TWO HUNDRED TWENTY-TWO

53 SEVERAL HUNDRED

82

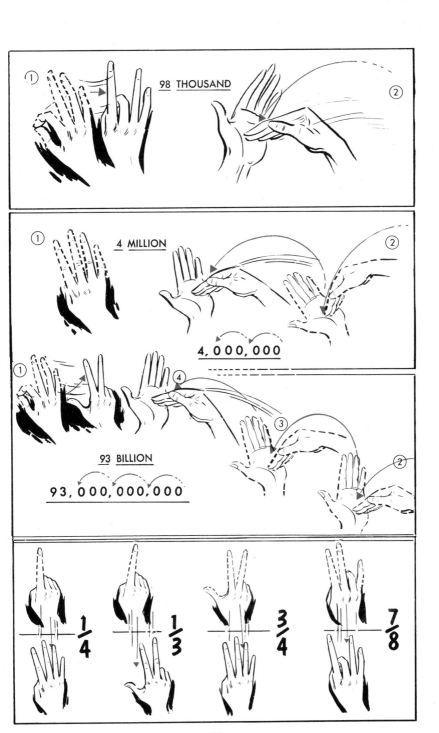

98 THOUSAND

4 MILLION

4,000,000

93 BILLION

93,000,000,000

$\frac{1}{4}$ $\frac{1}{3}$ $\frac{3}{4}$ $\frac{7}{8}$

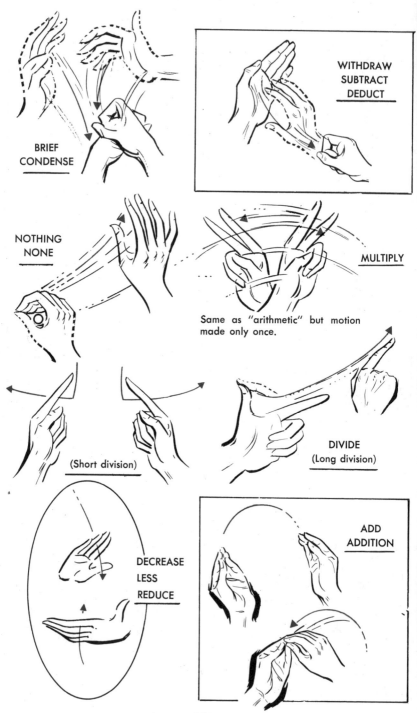

BRIEF
CONDENSE

WITHDRAW
SUBTRACT
DEDUCT

NOTHING
NONE

MULTIPLY

Same as "arithmetic" but motion
made only once.

(Short division)

DIVIDE
(Long division)

DECREASE
LESS
REDUCE

ADD
ADDITION

84

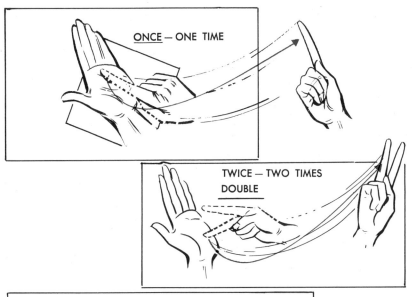

ONCE — ONE TIME

TWICE — TWO TIMES
DOUBLE

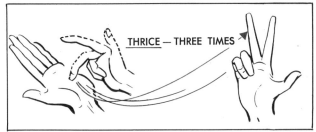

THRICE — THREE TIMES

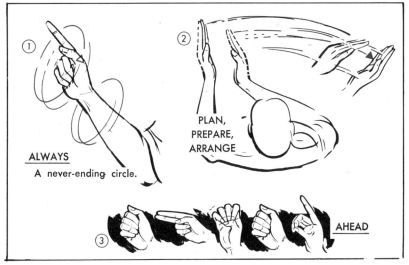

① ALWAYS
A never-ending circle.

② PLAN,
PREPARE,
ARRANGE

③ AHEAD

85

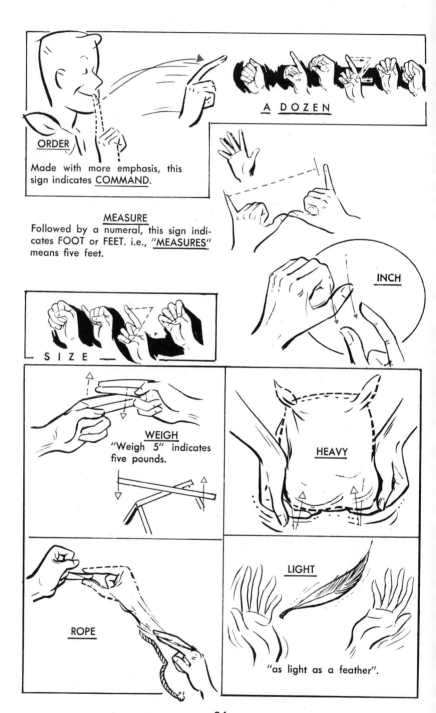

A DOZEN

ORDER

Made with more emphasis, this sign indicates COMMAND.

MEASURE

Followed by a numeral, this sign indicates FOOT or FEET. i.e., "MEASURES" means five feet.

INCH

SIZE

WEIGH

"Weigh 5" indicates five pounds.

HEAVY

ROPE

LIGHT

"as light as a feather".

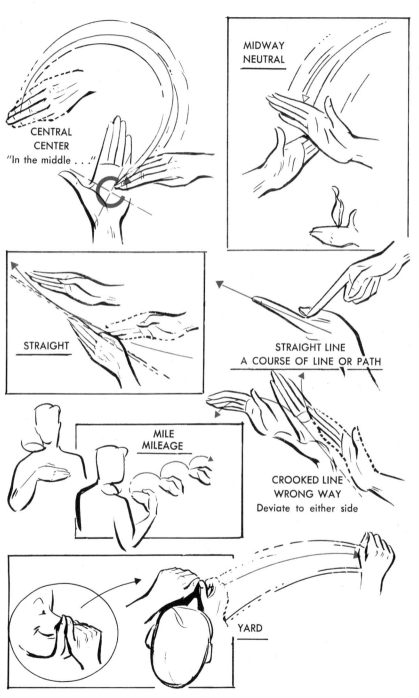

CENTRAL
CENTER
"In the middle . . ."

MIDWAY
NEUTRAL

STRAIGHT

STRAIGHT LINE
A COURSE OF LINE OR PATH

MILE
MILEAGE

CROOKED LINE
WRONG WAY
Deviate to either side

YARD

Family

CAMERA . . . Imitate shooting a candid camera.

CLICK!

FAMILY

The letters F.

KISS

HUG

GIRL

The sign indicates *female sex* and is the basic sign for woman, mother, lady, etc., as will be seen. It comes from the old days when women wore sunbonnets. The thumb drawn across the side of the face traces the bonnet ribbon.

<u>Male.</u> The sign indicates a man tipping his hat.

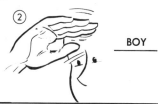

BOY

MOTHER

This is the sign for BABY. A mother is a girl (or female) who holds a baby, a combination of the sign for GIRL and BABY.

1 and 3 ... MOTHER
2 and 3 ... FATHER
1 and 4 ... GRANDMOTHER
2 and 4 ... GRANDFATHER

(See page 173)

A <u>FATHER</u> is a male who holds a baby

A <u>GRANDMOTHER</u> is a female who has held two babies so the sign for BABY is made twice.

<u>GRANDFATHER</u> holds two babies.

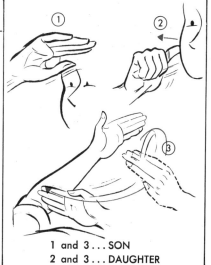

1 and 3 ... SON
2 and 3 ... DAUGHTER

89

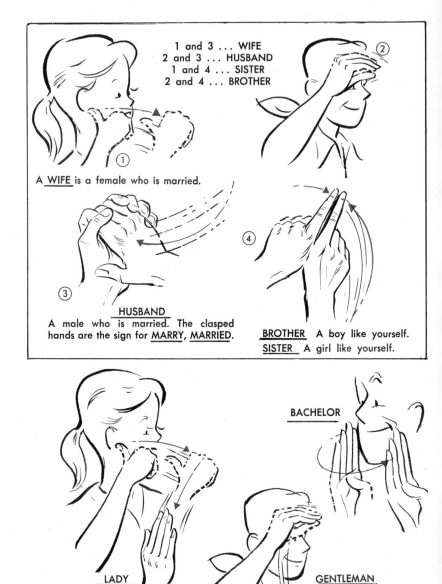

1 and 3 ... WIFE
2 and 3 ... HUSBAND
1 and 4 ... SISTER
2 and 4 ... BROTHER

A WIFE is a female who is married.

HUSBAND
A male who is married. The clasped hands are the sign for MARRY, MARRIED.

BROTHER A boy like yourself.
SISTER A girl like yourself.

BACHELOR

LADY
The open hand in front of the chest indicates ruffles ladies used to wear. It is the sign for POLITE or COURTEOUS. A LADY is a polite female.

GENTLEMAN

A polite male.

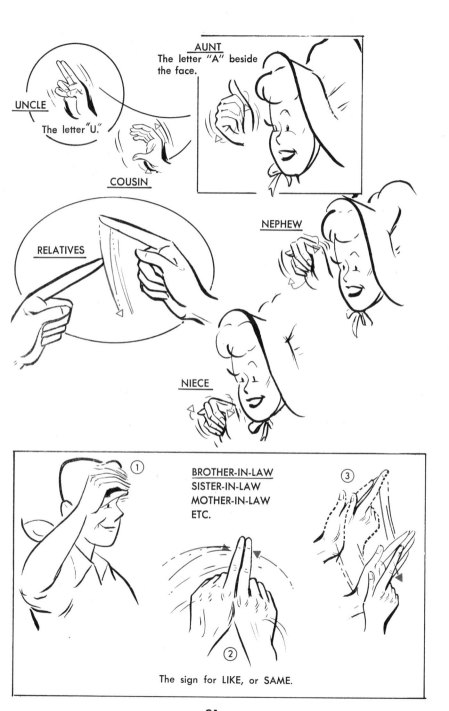

UNCLE
The letter "U."

AUNT
The letter "A" beside the face.

COUSIN

RELATIVES

NEPHEW

NIECE

BROTHER-IN-LAW
SISTER-IN-LAW
MOTHER-IN-LAW
ETC.

The sign for LIKE, or SAME.

CHURCH
CHAPEL

RELIGION

Religion

GOD

WORSHIP

(Showing the scars on His hands.)

JESUS

HOLY

THE BIBLE (Jesus' Book)

SOUL
SPIRIT (also GHOST)

SHEPHERD

1, 2 and 3 . . .

HOLY SPIRIT

MISSED

YOU

WE

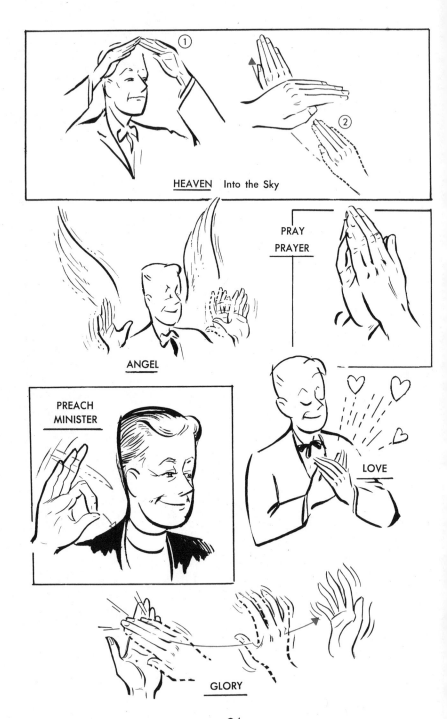

HEAVEN   Into the Sky

PRAY
PRAYER

ANGEL

PREACH
MINISTER

LOVE

GLORY

94

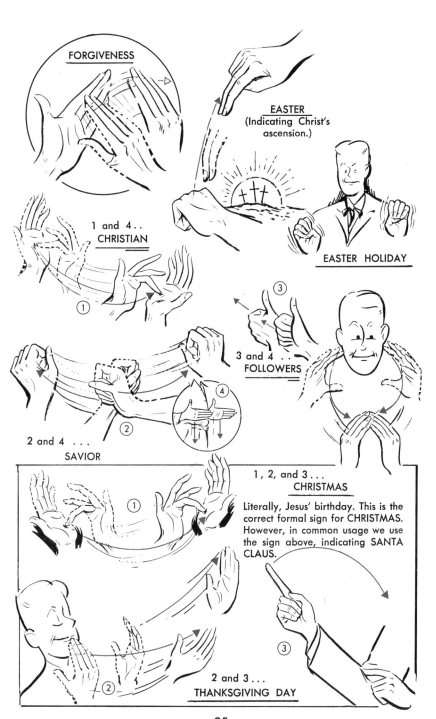

FORGIVENESS

EASTER
(Indicating Christ's ascension.)

EASTER HOLIDAY

1 and 4..
CHRISTIAN

3 and 4 ..
FOLLOWERS

2 and 4 . . .
SAVIOR

1, 2, and 3 . . .
CHRISTMAS

Literally, Jesus' birthday. This is the correct formal sign for CHRISTMAS. However, in common usage we use the sign above, indicating SANTA CLAUS.

2 and 3 . . .
THANKSGIVING DAY

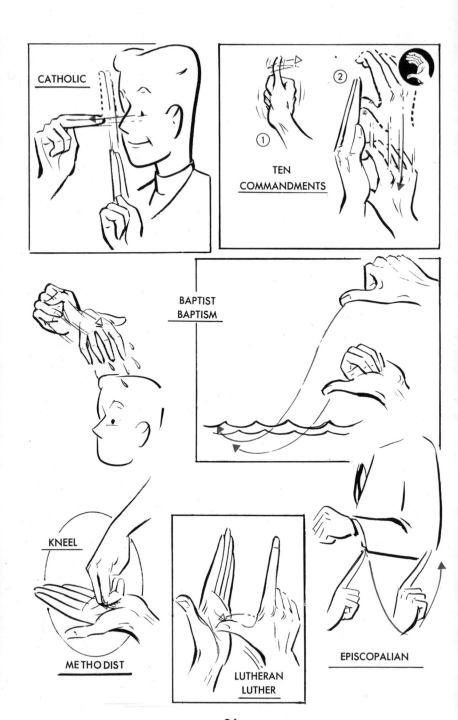

CATHOLIC

TEN COMMANDMENTS

① ②

BAPTIST BAPTISM

KNEEL

METHODIST

LUTHERAN LUTHER

EPISCOPALIAN

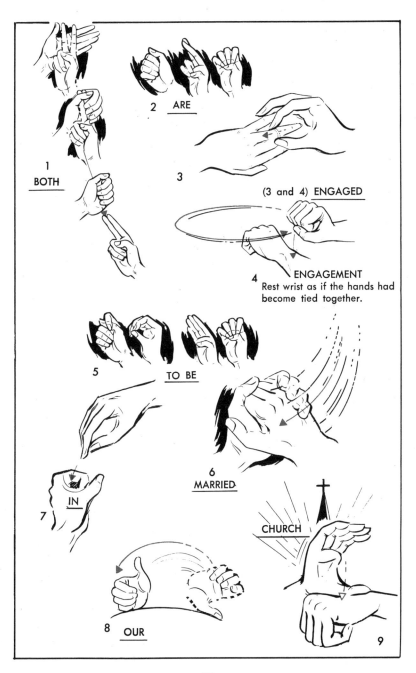

1
BOTH

2 ARE

3

(3 and 4) ENGAGED

4 ENGAGEMENT
Rest wrist as if the hands had
become tied together.

5 TO BE

6
MARRIED

7 IN

CHURCH

8 OUR

9

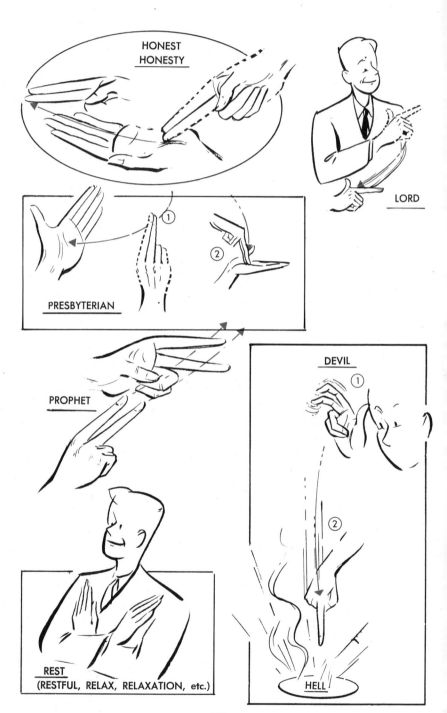

HONEST
HONESTY

LORD

PRESBYTERIAN

PROPHET

DEVIL

REST
(RESTFUL, RELAX, RELAXATION, etc.)

HELL

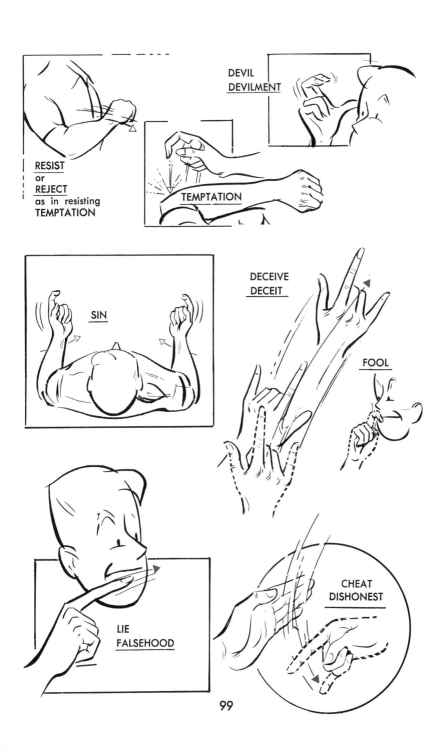

RESIST
or
REJECT
as in resisting
TEMPTATION

DEVIL
DEVILMENT

TEMPTATION

SIN

DECEIVE
DECEIT

FOOL

LIE
FALSEHOOD

CHEAT
DISHONEST

99

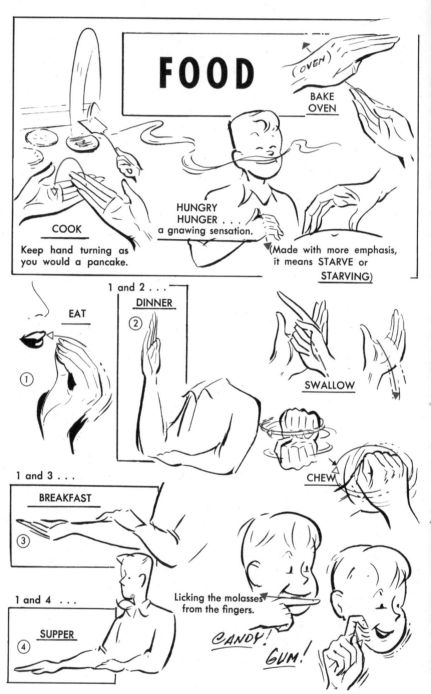

FOOD

BAKE OVEN

COOK
Keep hand turning as you would a pancake.

HUNGRY HUNGER . . . a gnawing sensation.

(Made with more emphasis, it means STARVE or STARVING)

EAT
①

1 and 2 . . .
DINNER
②

SWALLOW

CHEW

1 and 3 . . .
BREAKFAST
③

1 and 4 . . .
SUPPER
④

Licking the molasses from the fingers.

CANDY!

GUM!

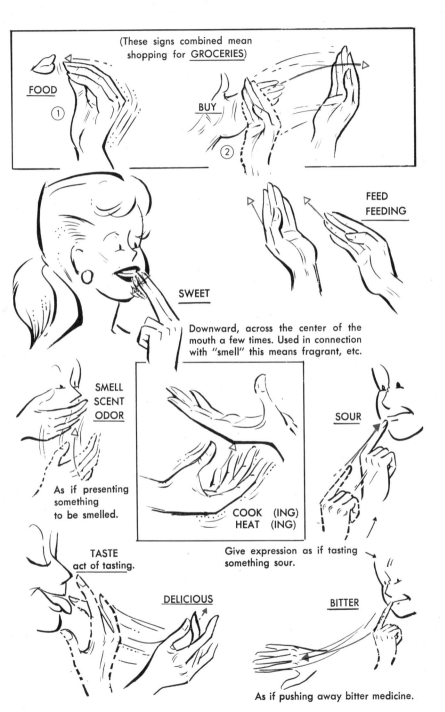

(These signs combined mean
shopping for GROCERIES)

FOOD
①

BUY
②

FEED
FEEDING

SWEET

Downward, across the center of the
mouth a few times. Used in connection
with "smell" this means fragrant, etc.

SMELL
SCENT
ODOR

As if presenting
something
to be smelled.

COOK   (ING)
HEAT   (ING)

SOUR

Give expression as if tasting
something sour.

TASTE
act of tasting.

DELICIOUS

BITTER

As if pushing away bitter medicine.

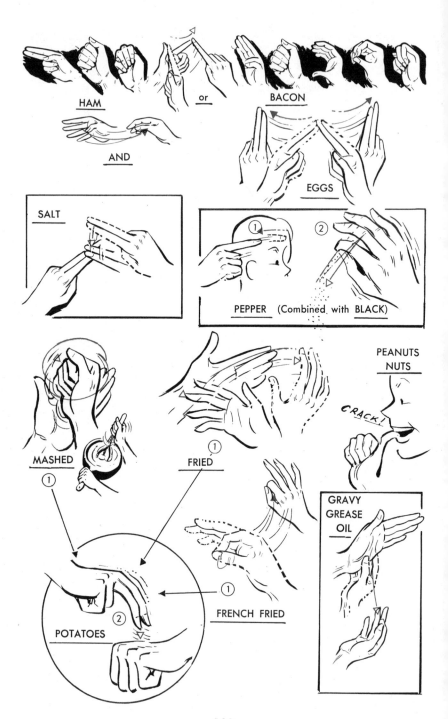

HAM

or

BACON

AND

EGGS

SALT

PEPPER (Combined with BLACK)

MASHED

FRIED

PEANUTS
NUTS

CRACK!

POTATOES

FRENCH FRIED

GRAVY
GREASE
OIL

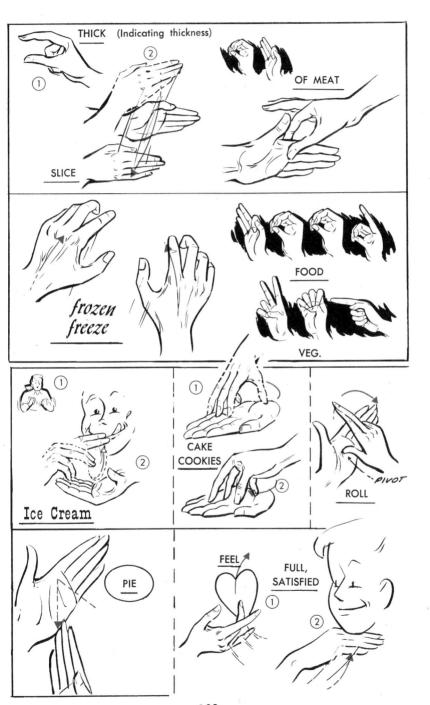

THICK (Indicating thickness)

① ②

OF MEAT

SLICE

frozen freeze

FOOD

VEG.

Ice Cream ① ②

CAKE COOKIES ① ②

ROLL *PIVOT*

PIE

FEEL FULL, SATISFIED ① ②

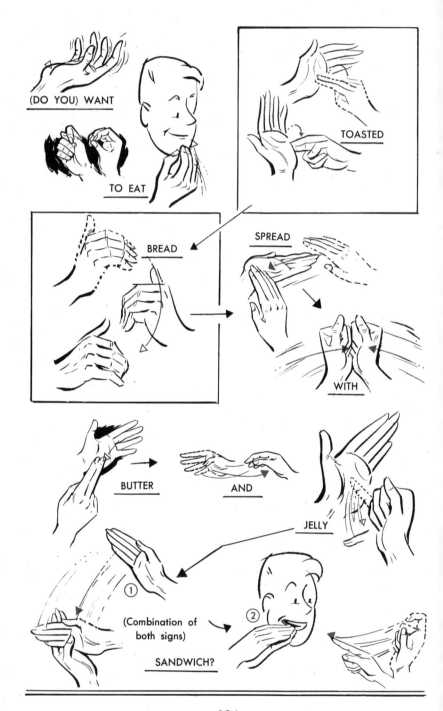

(DO YOU) WANT

TO EAT

TOASTED

BREAD

SPREAD

WITH

BUTTER

AND

JELLY

① (Combination of both signs) ②

SANDWICH?

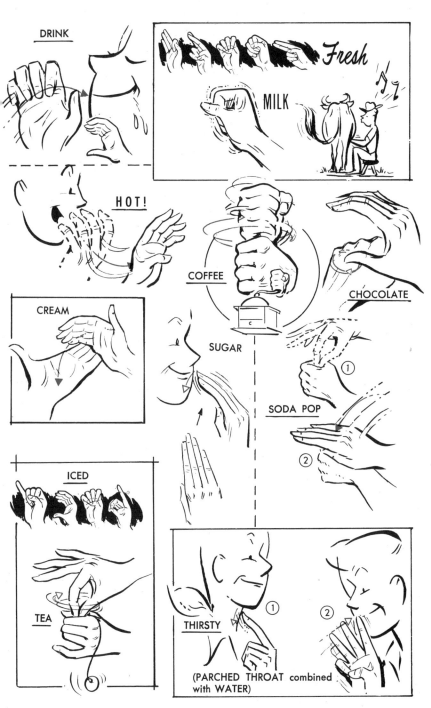

DRINK

Fresh

MILK

HOT!

COFFEE

CHOCOLATE

CREAM

SUGAR

SODA POP
①
②

ICED

TEA

THIRSTY
① ②

(PARCHED THROAT combined with WATER)

105

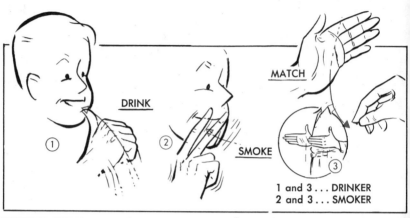

DRINK ①

SMOKE ②

MATCH

③

1 and 3 . . . DRINKER
2 and 3 . . . SMOKER

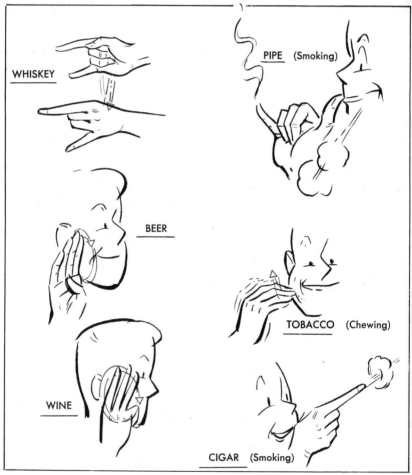

WHISKEY

PIPE (Smoking)

BEER

TOBACCO (Chewing)

WINE

CIGAR (Smoking)

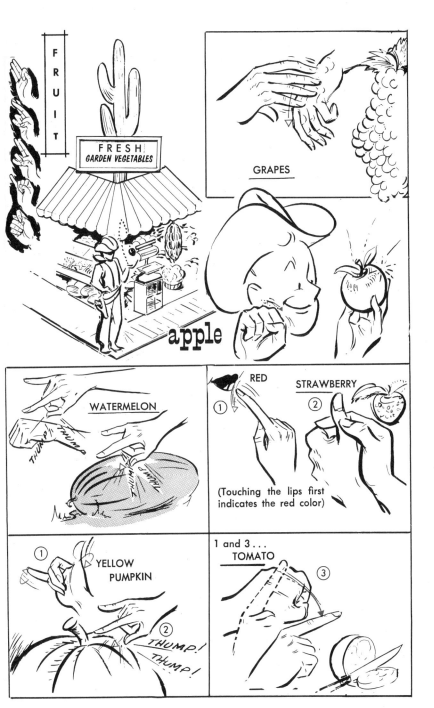

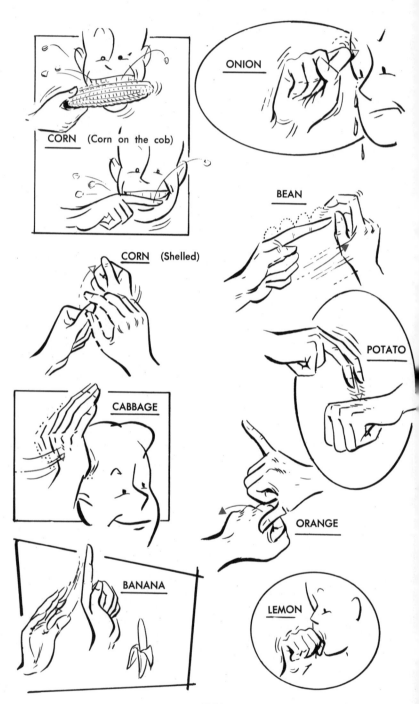

CORN (Corn on the cob)

ONION

CORN (Shelled)

BEAN

CABBAGE

POTATO

BANANA

ORANGE

LEMON

108

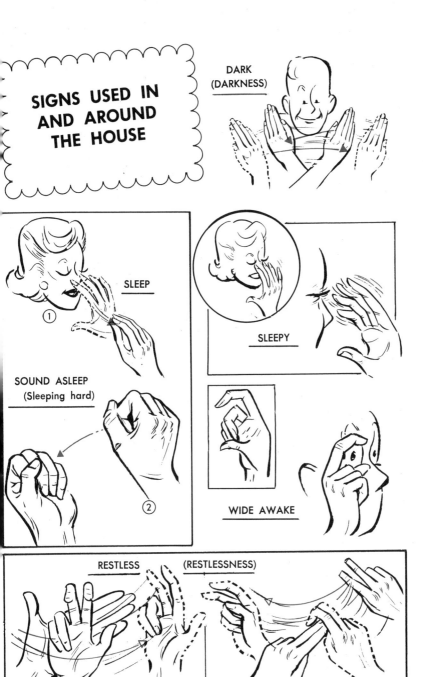

SIGNS USED IN AND AROUND THE HOUSE

DARK (DARKNESS)

SLEEP ①

SLEEPY

SOUND ASLEEP (Sleeping hard) ②

WIDE AWAKE

RESTLESS (RESTLESSNESS)

Tossing in bed or squirming on a seat.

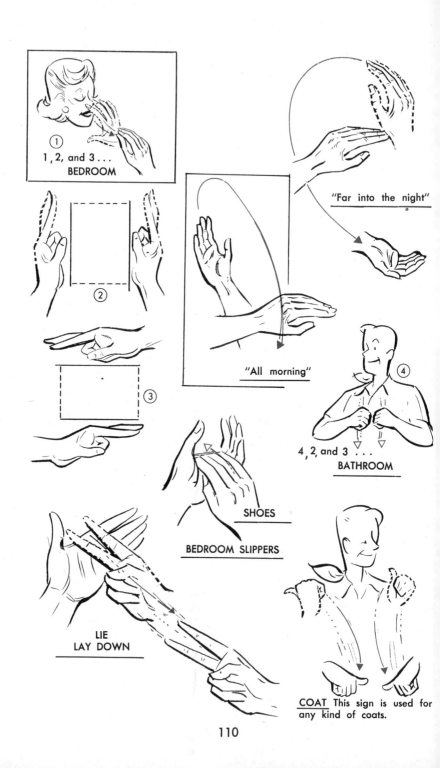

① 1, 2, and 3 . . .
BEDROOM

②

③

"Far into the night"

"All morning"

SHOES

BEDROOM SLIPPERS

④ 4, 2, and 3 . . .
BATHROOM

LIE
LAY DOWN

COAT This sign is used for
any kind of coats.

110

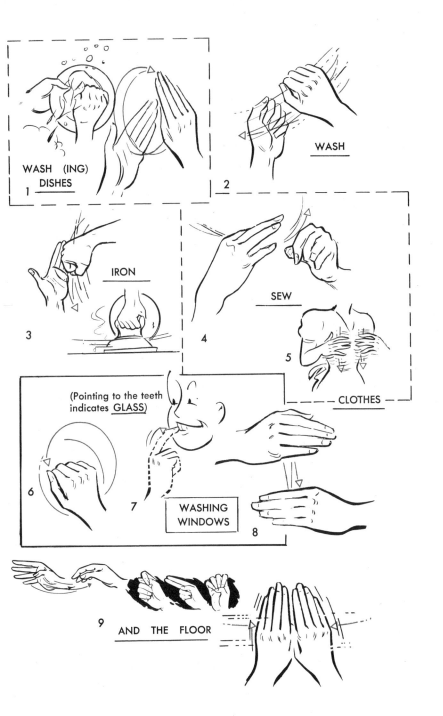

WASH (ING) DISHES
1

WASH
2

IRON
3

SEW
4

5

CLOTHES

(Pointing to the teeth indicates GLASS)
6

7

WASHING WINDOWS
8

9 **AND THE FLOOR**

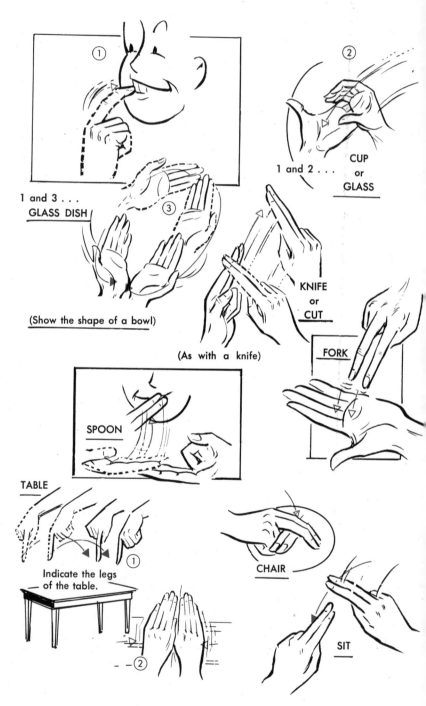

1 and 2 . . . CUP or GLASS

1 and 3 . . . GLASS DISH

(Show the shape of a bowl)

KNIFE or CUT

(As with a knife)

FORK

SPOON

TABLE

Indicate the legs of the table.

CHAIR

SIT

112

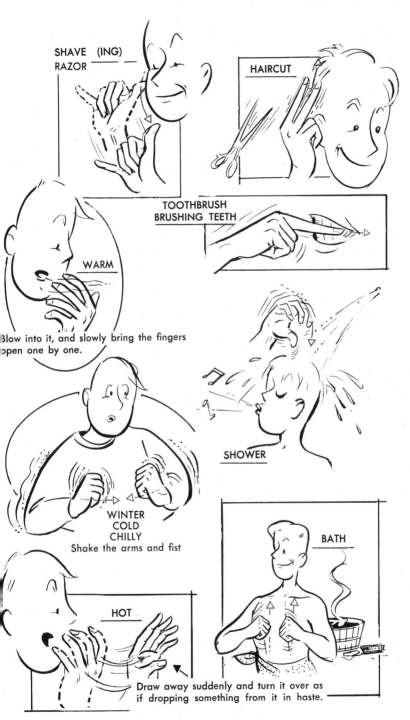

SHAVE (ING)
RAZOR

HAIRCUT

TOOTHBRUSH
BRUSHING TEETH

WARM

Blow into it, and slowly bring the fingers
open one by one.

SHOWER

WINTER
COLD
CHILLY
Shake the arms and fist

BATH

HOT

Draw away suddenly and turn it over as
if dropping something from it in haste.

113

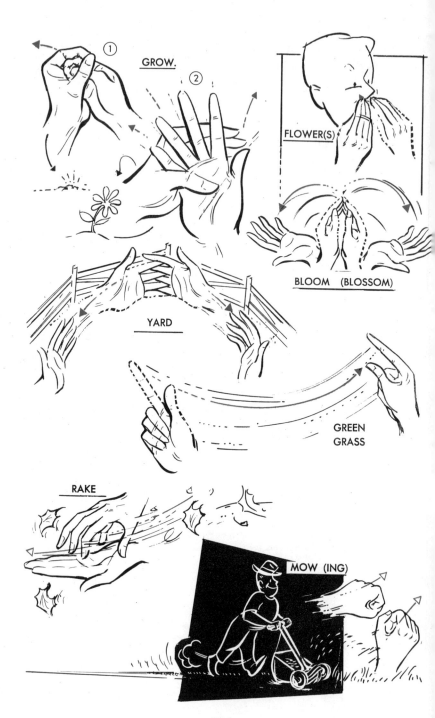

GROW.
① ②

FLOWER(S)

BLOOM (BLOSSOM)

YARD

GREEN GRASS

RAKE

MOW (ING)

114

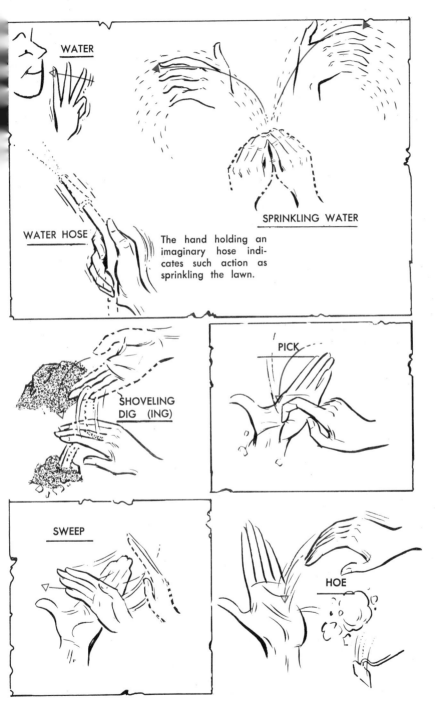

WATER

SPRINKLING WATER

WATER HOSE

The hand holding an imaginary hose indicates such action as sprinkling the lawn.

SHOVELING DIG (ING)

PICK

SWEEP

HOE

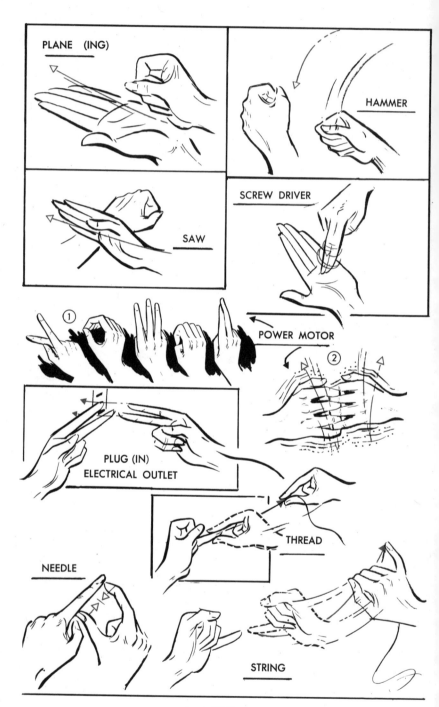

PLANE (ING)

HAMMER

SAW

SCREW DRIVER

POWER MOTOR

PLUG (IN)
ELECTRICAL OUTLET

THREAD

NEEDLE

STRING

116

ILLNESS
AND
MEDICINE

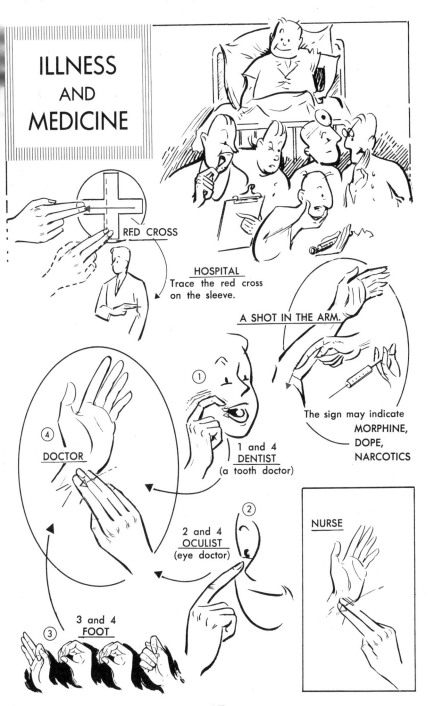

RED CROSS

HOSPITAL
Trace the red cross
on the sleeve.

A SHOT IN THE ARM.

The sign may indicate
MORPHINE,
DOPE,
NARCOTICS

① 1 and 4
DENTIST
(a tooth doctor)

④ DOCTOR

② 2 and 4
OCULIST
(eye doctor)

NURSE

③ 3 and 4
FOOT

117

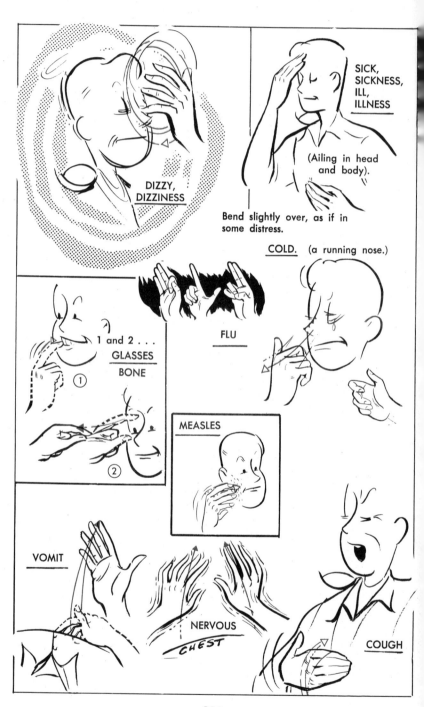

DIZZY, DIZZINESS

SICK, SICKNESS, ILL, ILLNESS

(Ailing in head and body).

Bend slightly over, as if in some distress.

COLD. (a running nose.)

1 and 2 . . . GLASSES
BONE
①
②

FLU

MEASLES

VOMIT

NERVOUS

CHEST

COUGH

118

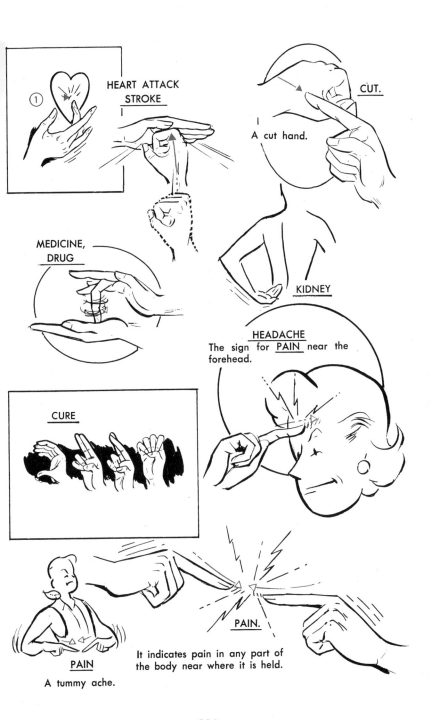

① HEART ATTACK
STROKE

CUT.

A cut hand.

MEDICINE,
DRUG

KIDNEY

HEADACHE
The sign for PAIN near the forehead.

CURE

PAIN.
It indicates pain in any part of the body near where it is held.

PAIN
A tummy ache.

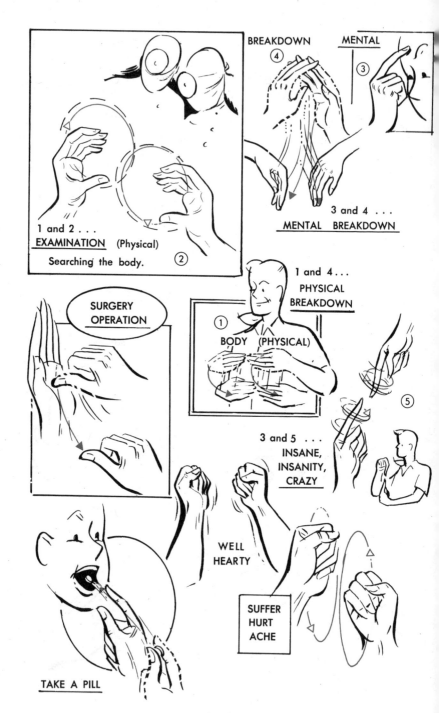

BREAKDOWN ④ MENTAL ③

3 and 4 . . .
MENTAL BREAKDOWN

1 and 2 . . .
EXAMINATION (Physical)
Searching the body. ②

1 and 4 . . .
PHYSICAL BREAKDOWN

SURGERY OPERATION

① BODY (PHYSICAL)

3 and 5 . . .
INSANE, INSANITY, CRAZY ⑤

WELL HEARTY

SUFFER HURT ACHE

TAKE A PILL

120

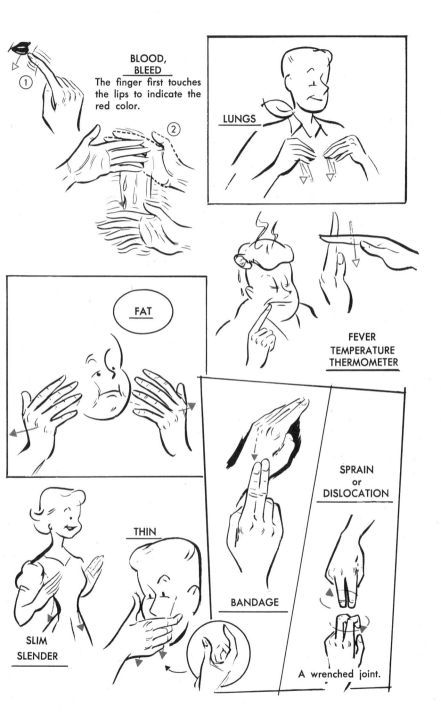

BLOOD, BLEED
The finger first touches the lips to indicate the red color.

LUNGS

FAT

FEVER
TEMPERATURE
THERMOMETER

BANDAGE

SPRAIN
or
DISLOCATION

THIN

SLIM
SLENDER

A wrenched joint.

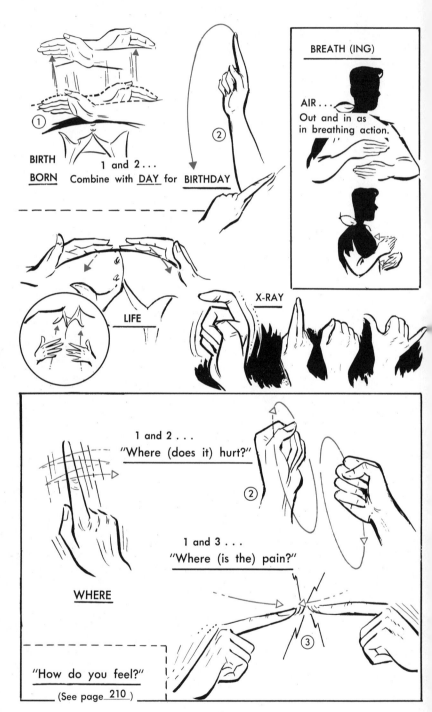

BREATH (ING)

BIRTH
BORN 1 and 2... Combine with DAY for BIRTHDAY

AIR...
Out and in as
in breathing action.

LIFE

X-RAY

1 and 2 . . .
"Where (does it) hurt?"

1 and 3 . . .
"Where (is the) pain?"

WHERE

"How do you feel?"
(See page 210)

122

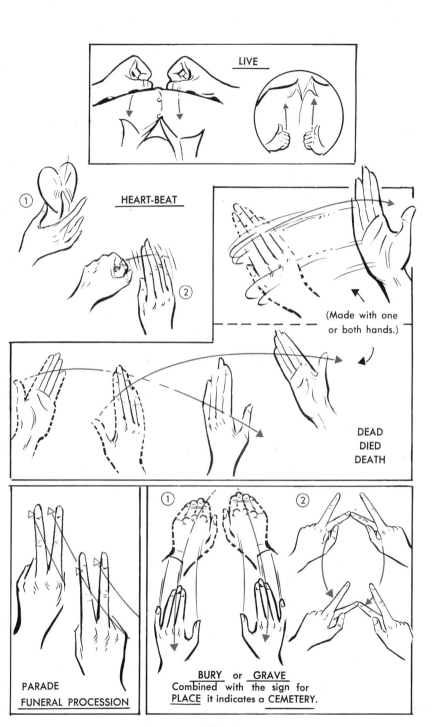

LIVE

HEART-BEAT

(Made with one or both hands.)

DEAD
DIED
DEATH

PARADE
FUNERAL PROCESSION

BURY or GRAVE
Combined with the sign for
PLACE it indicates a CEMETERY.

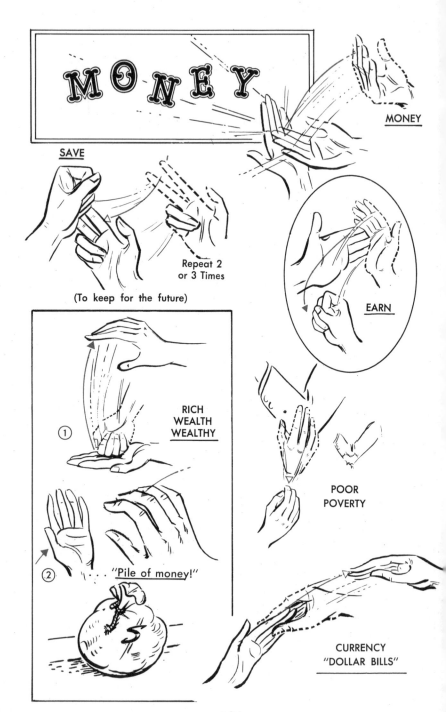

MONEY

MONEY

SAVE

Repeat 2
or 3 Times

(To keep for the future)

EARN

RICH
WEALTH
WEALTHY

①

②

"Pile of money!"

POOR
POVERTY

CURRENCY
"DOLLAR BILLS"

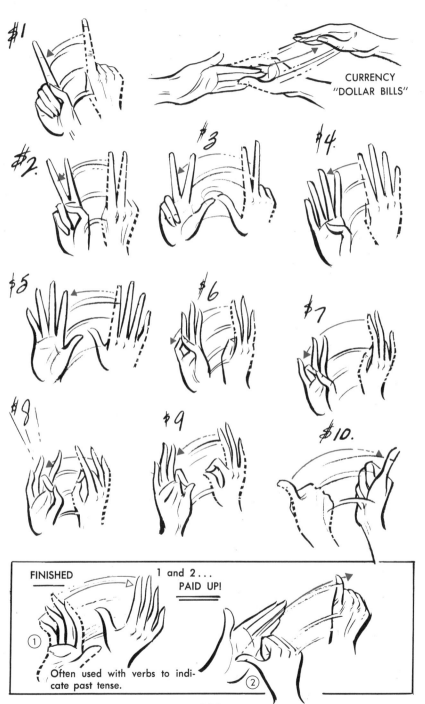

#1

CURRENCY
"DOLLAR BILLS"

#2.

#3

#4.

$5

$6

$7

$8

$9

$10.

FINISHED

1 and 2 ...
PAID UP!

① Often used with verbs to indicate past tense.

②

125

SIGNATURE
SIGN

"Sign your name", or
"Put your signature here."

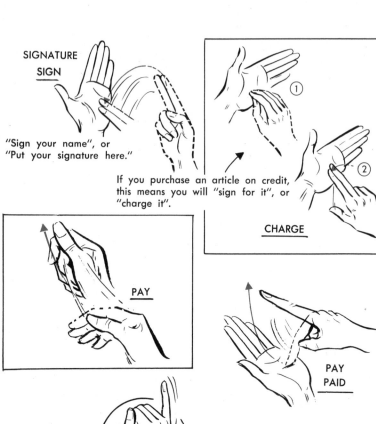

If you purchase an article on credit,
this means you will "sign for it", or
"charge it".

CHARGE

PAY

PAY
PAID

INSURANCE

RAISE
GAIN
INCREASE

PROFIT

Stick the money into
your vest pocket.

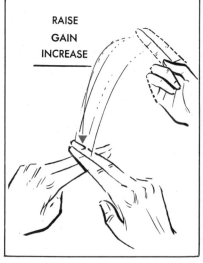

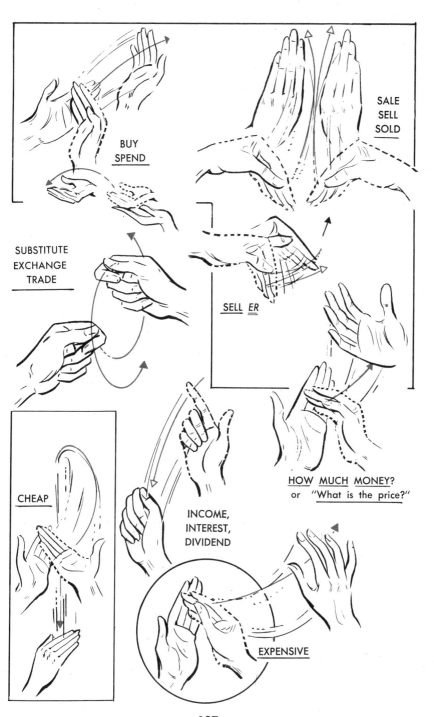

BUY
SPEND

SALE
SELL
SOLD

SUBSTITUTE
EXCHANGE
TRADE

SELL _ER_

CHEAP

INCOME,
INTEREST,
DIVIDEND

HOW MUCH MONEY?
or "What is the price?"

EXPENSIVE

127

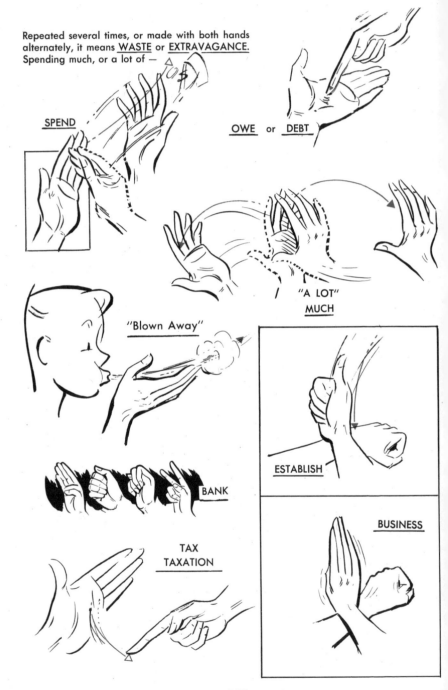

Repeated several times, or made with both hands alternately, it means <u>WASTE</u> or <u>EXTRAVAGANCE.</u> Spending much, or a lot of —

<u>SPEND</u>

<u>OWE</u> or <u>DEBT</u>

"A LOT"
<u>MUCH</u>

"Blown Away"

<u>ESTABLISH</u>

<u>BUSINESS</u>

<u>BANK</u>

TAX
<u>TAXATION</u>

128

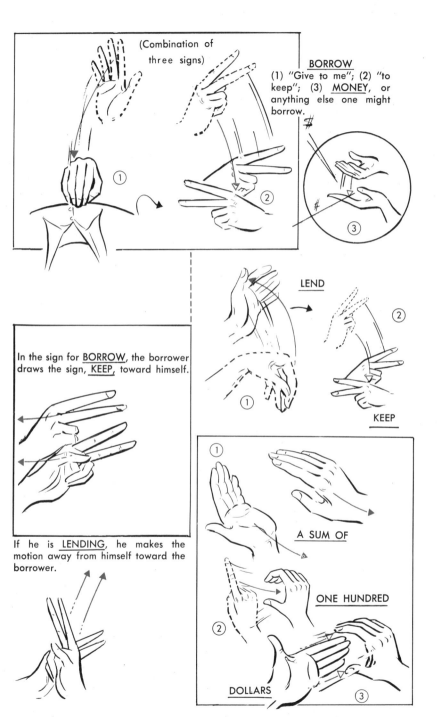

(Combination of three signs)

BORROW
(1) "Give to me"; (2) "to keep"; (3) MONEY, or anything else one might borrow.

LEND

KEEP

In the sign for BORROW, the borrower draws the sign, KEEP, toward himself.

If he is LENDING, he makes the motion away from himself toward the borrower.

A SUM OF

ONE HUNDRED

DOLLARS

129

OCCUPATIONS

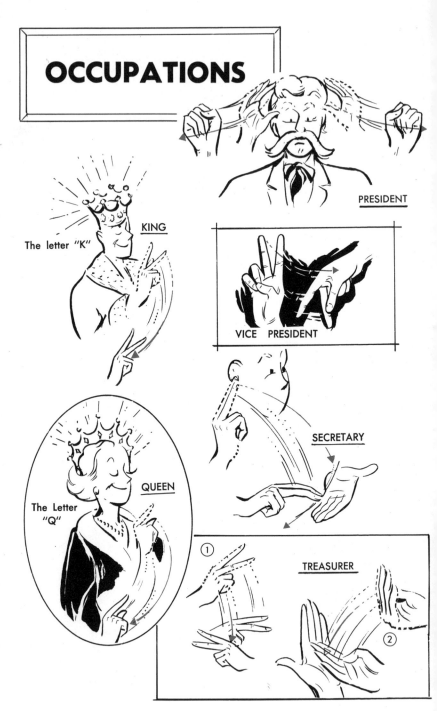

PRESIDENT

KING

The letter "K"

VICE PRESIDENT

SECRETARY

QUEEN

The Letter "Q"

① TREASURER ②

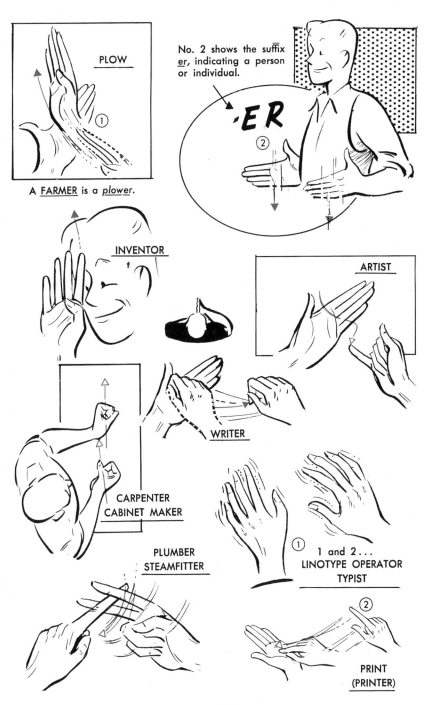

PLOW

No. 2 shows the suffix _er_, indicating a person or individual.

'ER

②

A FARMER is a _plower_.

INVENTOR

ARTIST

WRITER

CARPENTER
CABINET MAKER

PLUMBER
STEAMFITTER

① 1 and 2...
LINOTYPE OPERATOR
TYPIST

②

PRINT
(PRINTER)

131

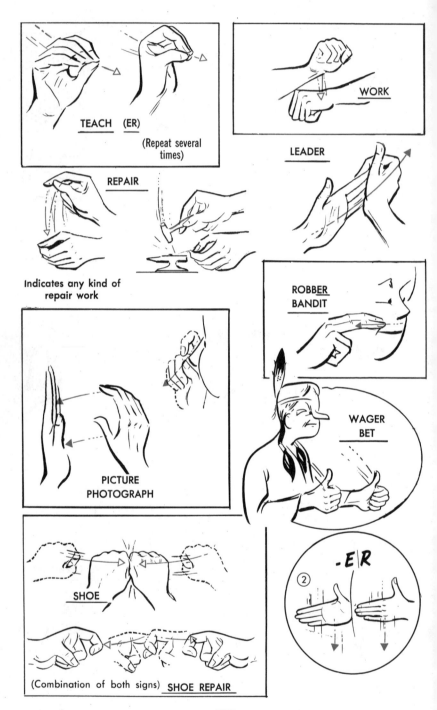

TEACH (ER)

(Repeat several times)

WORK

LEADER

REPAIR

Indicates any kind of repair work

ROBBER BANDIT

PICTURE PHOTOGRAPH

WAGER BET

SHOE

-E\R

②

(Combination of both signs) SHOE REPAIR

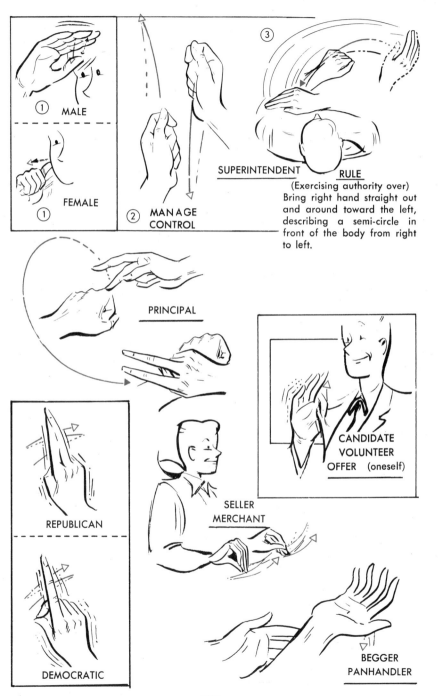

① MALE

① FEMALE

② MANAGE
CONTROL

③

SUPERINTENDENT

RULE
(Exercising authority over)
Bring right hand straight out
and around toward the left,
describing a semi-circle in
front of the body from right
to left.

PRINCIPAL

CANDIDATE
VOLUNTEER
OFFER (oneself)

REPUBLICAN

DEMOCRATIC

SELLER
MERCHANT

BEGGER
PANHANDLER

133

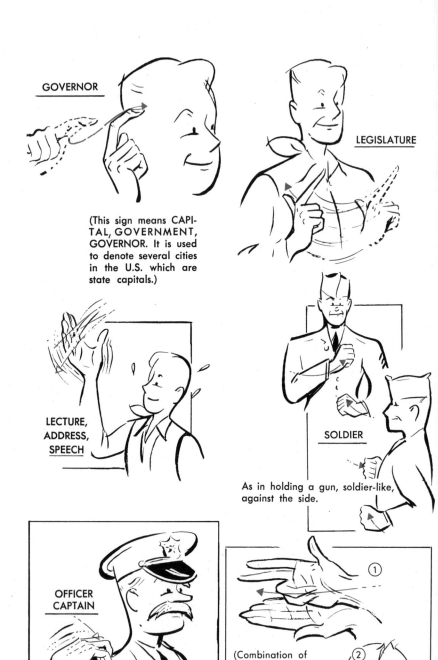

GOVERNOR

(This sign means CAPITAL, GOVERNMENT, GOVERNOR. It is used to denote several cities in the U.S. which are state capitals.)

LEGISLATURE

LECTURE, ADDRESS, SPEECH

SOLDIER

As in holding a gun, soldier-like, against the side.

OFFICER CAPTAIN

(Combination of both signs)

① ②

SAILOR

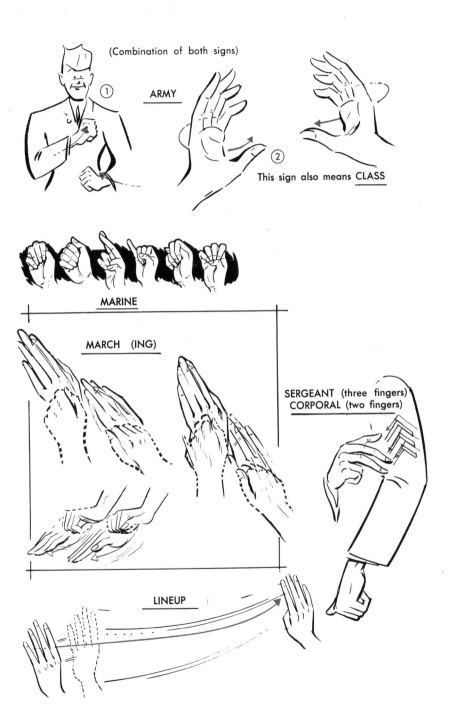

(Combination of both signs)

ARMY

① ②

This sign also means CLASS

MARINE

MARCH (ING)

SERGEANT (three fingers)
CORPORAL (two fingers)

LINEUP

135

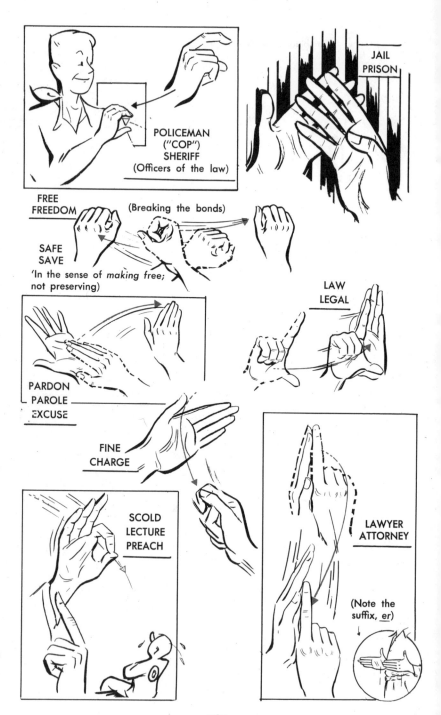

POLICEMAN
("COP")
SHERIFF
(Officers of the law)

JAIL
PRISON

FREE
FREEDOM

(Breaking the bonds)

SAFE
SAVE

'In the sense of *making free*; not preserving)

LAW
LEGAL

PARDON
PAROLE
EXCUSE

FINE
CHARGE

SCOLD
LECTURE
PREACH

LAWYER
ATTORNEY

(Note the suffix, _er_)

136

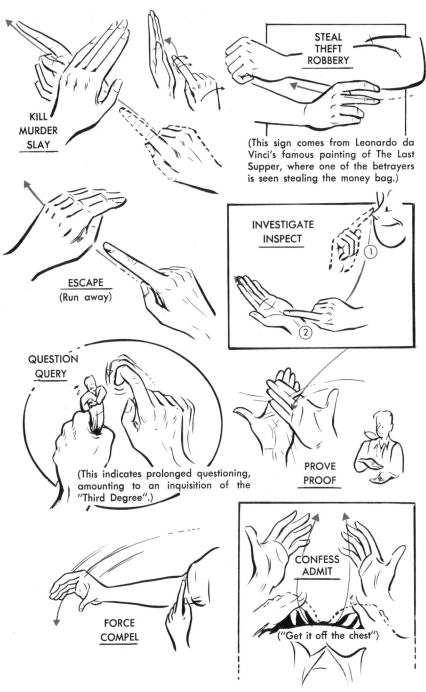

KILL
MURDER
SLAY

STEAL
THEFT
ROBBERY

(This sign comes from Leonardo da Vinci's famous painting of The Last Supper, where one of the betrayers is seen stealing the money bag.)

ESCAPE
(Run away)

INVESTIGATE
INSPECT

QUESTION
QUERY

(This indicates prolonged questioning, amounting to an inquisition of the "Third Degree".)

PROVE
PROOF

FORCE
COMPEL

CONFESS
ADMIT

("Get it off the chest")

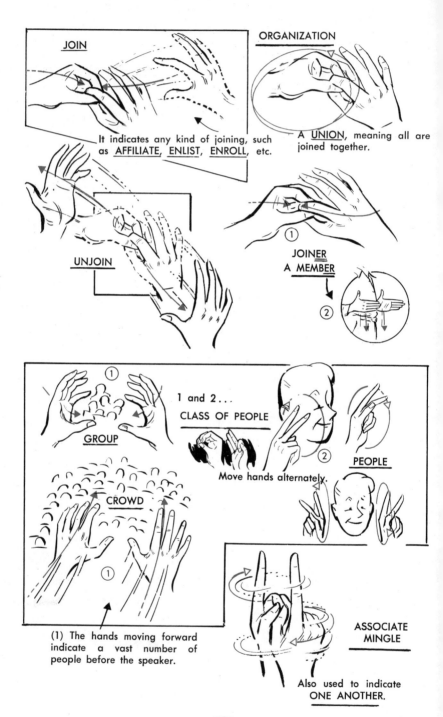

JOIN

It indicates any kind of joining, such as AFFILIATE, ENLIST, ENROLL, etc.

ORGANIZATION

A UNION, meaning all are joined together.

UNJOIN

JOINER
A MEMBER

GROUP

1 and 2...
CLASS OF PEOPLE

Move hands alternately.

PEOPLE

CROWD

(1) The hands moving forward indicate a vast number of people before the speaker.

ASSOCIATE
MINGLE

Also used to indicate
ONE ANOTHER.

138

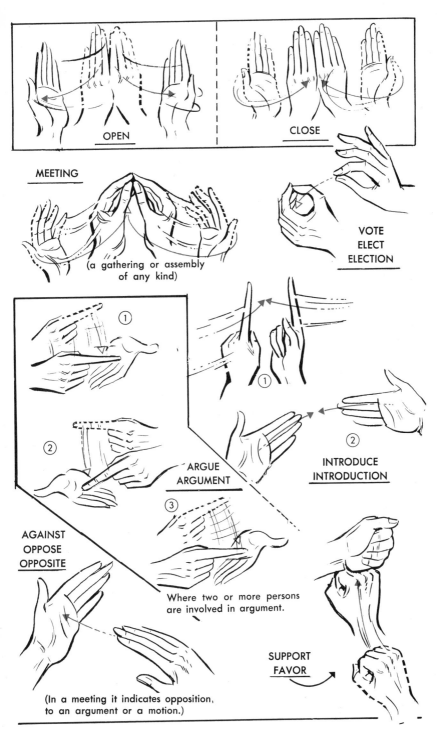

OPEN

CLOSE

MEETING

(a gathering or assembly of any kind)

VOTE
ELECT
ELECTION

① ①

② ②

ARGUE
ARGUMENT

INTRODUCE
INTRODUCTION

③

AGAINST
OPPOSE
OPPOSITE

Where two or more persons are involved in argument.

SUPPORT
FAVOR

(In a meeting it indicates opposition, to an argument or a motion.)

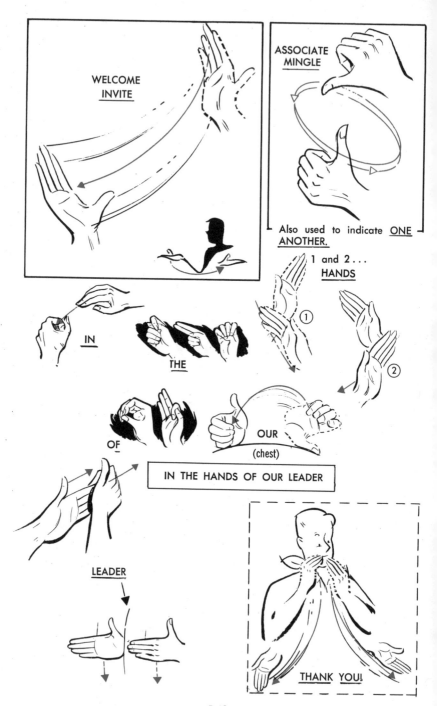

WELCOME
INVITE

ASSOCIATE
MINGLE

Also used to indicate ONE ANOTHER.

1 and 2 . . .
HANDS

①

②

IN

THE

OF

OUR
(chest)

IN THE HANDS OF OUR LEADER

LEADER

THANK YOU!

THE WORLD AND NATURE

LIGHT or BRIGHTNESS;
BRILLIANCE

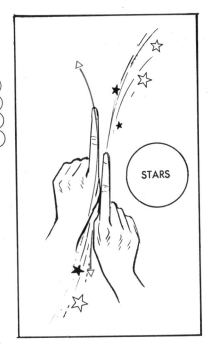

STARS

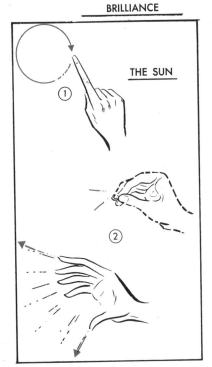

THE SUN

① ②

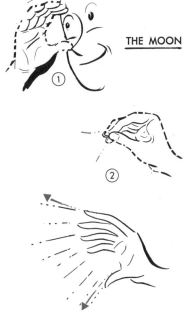

THE MOON

① ②

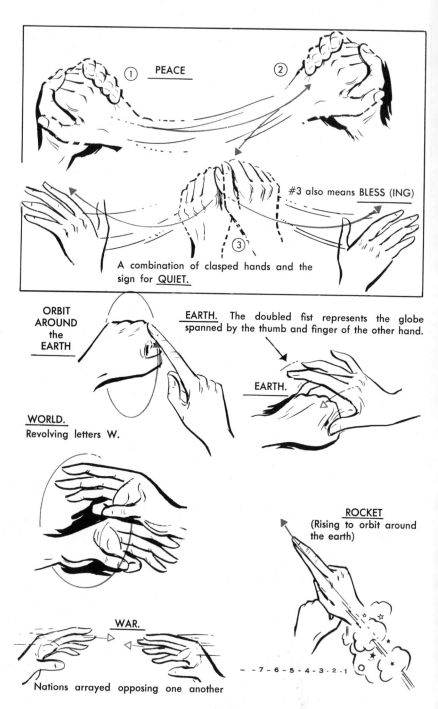

① PEACE ②

#3 also means BLESS (ING)

③

A combination of clasped hands and the sign for QUIET.

ORBIT AROUND the EARTH

EARTH. The doubled fist represents the globe spanned by the thumb and finger of the other hand.

EARTH.

WORLD. Revolving letters W.

ROCKET (Rising to orbit around the earth)

WAR. Nations arrayed opposing one another

- - 7 - 6 - 5 - 4 - 3 - 2 - 1 - 0

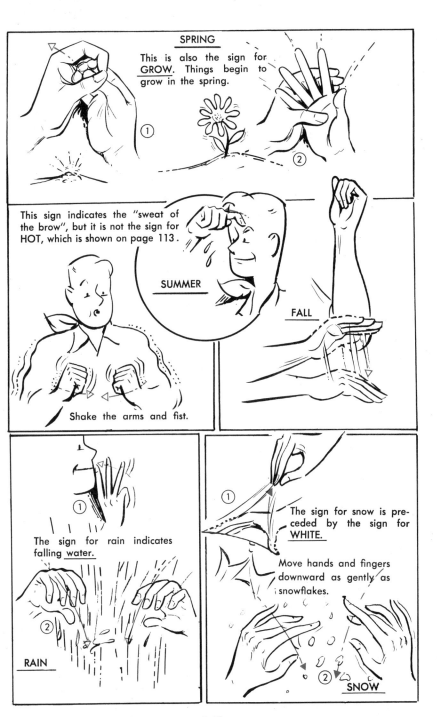

SPRING

This is also the sign for GROW. Things begin to grow in the spring.

① ②

This sign indicates the "sweat of the brow", but it is not the sign for HOT, which is shown on page 113.

SUMMER

FALL

Shake the arms and fist.

① The sign for rain indicates falling water.

②

RAIN

① The sign for snow is preceded by the sign for WHITE.

Move hands and fingers downward as gently as snowflakes.

② SNOW

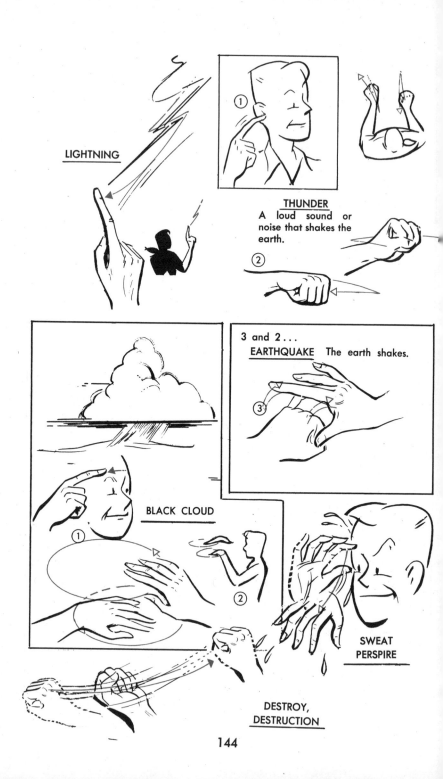

LIGHTNING

① THUNDER
A loud sound or noise that shakes the earth.

②

3 and 2...
EARTHQUAKE The earth shakes.
③

BLACK CLOUD
①
②

SWEAT
PERSPIRE

DESTROY,
DESTRUCTION

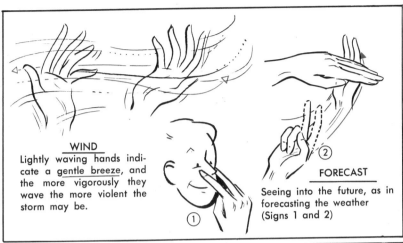

WIND

Lightly waving hands indicate a gentle breeze, and the more vigorously they wave the more violent the storm may be.

FORECAST

Seeing into the future, as in forecasting the weather (Signs 1 and 2)

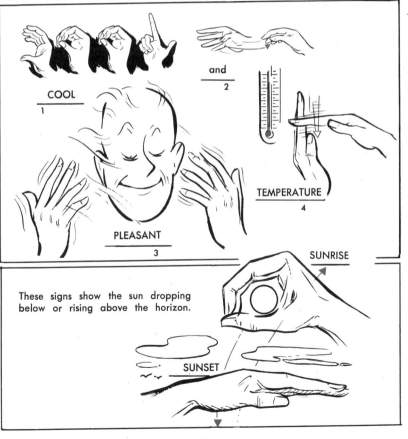

COOL
1

and
2

TEMPERATURE
4

PLEASANT
3

These signs show the sun dropping below or rising above the horizon.

SUNRISE

SUNSET

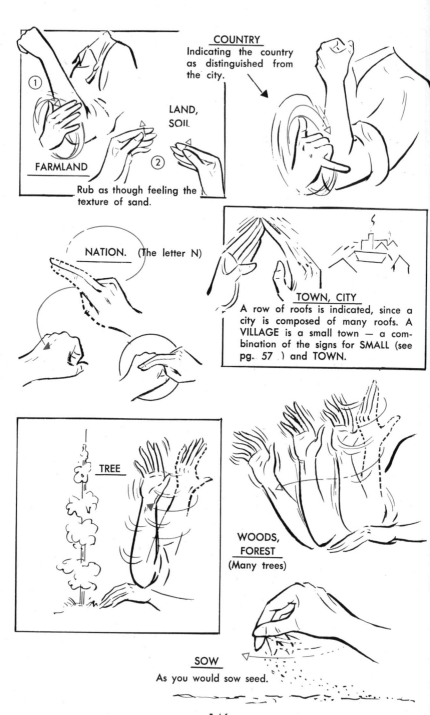

① FARMLAND
② LAND, SOIL

Rub as though feeling the texture of sand.

COUNTRY
Indicating the country as distinguished from the city.

NATION. (The letter N)

TOWN, CITY
A row of roofs is indicated, since a city is composed of many roofs. A VILLAGE is a small town — a combination of the signs for SMALL (see pg. 57) and TOWN.

TREE

WOODS, FOREST
(Many trees)

SOW
As you would sow seed.

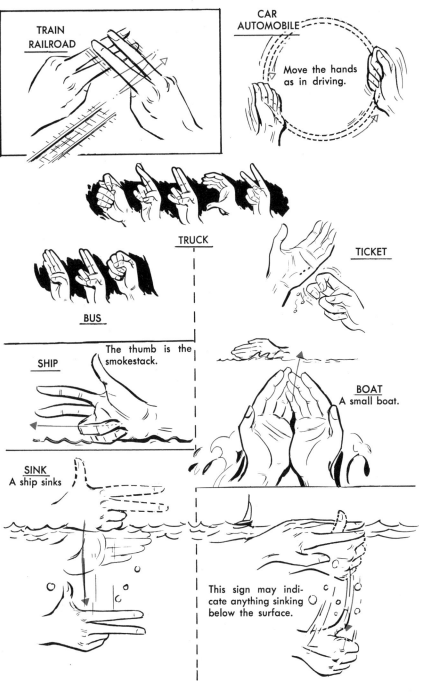

TRAIN
RAILROAD

CAR
AUTOMOBILE

Move the hands
as in driving.

TRUCK

TICKET

BUS

SHIP

The thumb is the
smokestack.

BOAT
A small boat.

SINK
A ship sinks

This sign may indi-
cate anything sinking
below the surface.

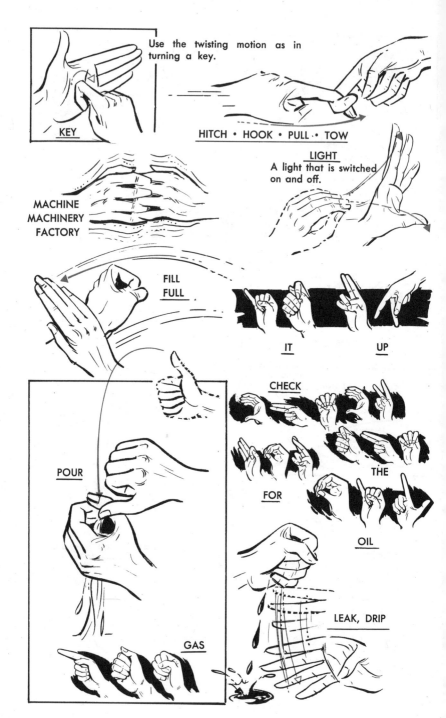

Use the twisting motion as in turning a key.

KEY

HITCH • HOOK • PULL • TOW

MACHINE MACHINERY FACTORY

LIGHT
A light that is switched on and off.

FILL FULL

IT   UP

CHECK

POUR

FOR

THE

OIL

LEAK, DRIP

GAS

148

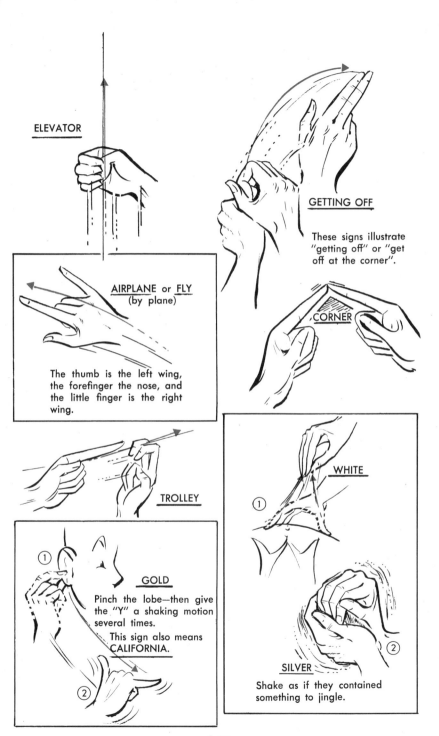

ELEVATOR

GETTING OFF

These signs illustrate "getting off" or "get off at the corner".

AIRPLANE or FLY
(by plane)

The thumb is the left wing, the forefinger the nose, and the little finger is the right wing.

CORNER

TROLLEY

WHITE

①

GOLD

Pinch the lobe—then give the "Y" a shaking motion several times.

This sign also means CALIFORNIA.

②

SILVER

Shake as if they contained something to jingle.

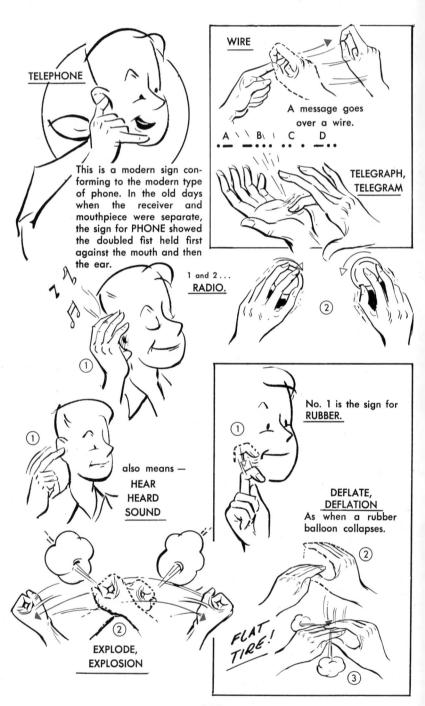

TELEPHONE

This is a modern sign conforming to the modern type of phone. In the old days when the receiver and mouthpiece were separate, the sign for PHONE showed the doubled fist held first against the mouth and then the ear.

WIRE

A message goes over a wire.

A   B   C   D

TELEGRAPH, TELEGRAM

1 and 2...
RADIO.

②

①

①

also means —
HEAR
HEARD
SOUND

No. 1 is the sign for RUBBER.

①

DEFLATE, DEFLATION
As when a rubber balloon collapses.

②

②
EXPLODE, EXPLOSION

FLAT TIRE!

③

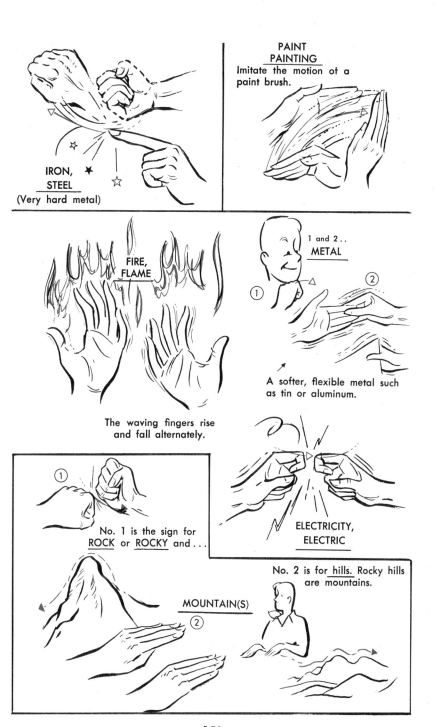

IRON,
STEEL
(Very hard metal)

PAINT
PAINTING
Imitate the motion of a
paint brush.

FIRE,
FLAME

The waving fingers rise
and fall alternately.

1 and 2..
METAL

A softer, flexible metal such
as tin or aluminum.

No. 1 is the sign for
ROCK or ROCKY and ...

ELECTRICITY,
ELECTRIC

MOUNTAIN(S)

No. 2 is for hills. Rocky hills
are mountains.

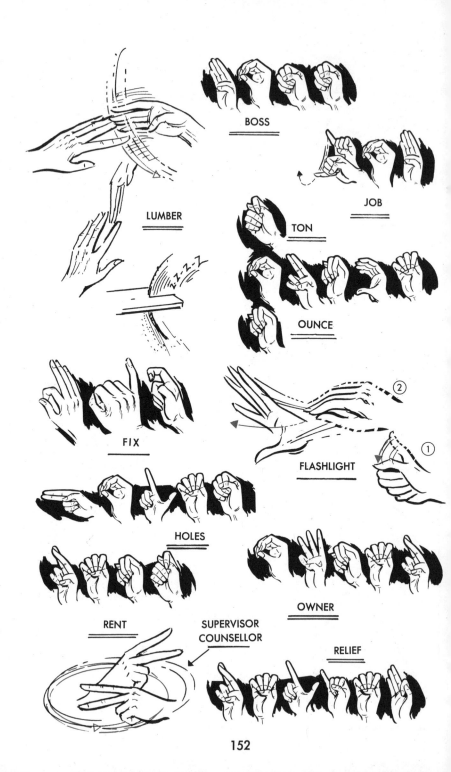

BOSS

JOB

LUMBER

TON

OUNCE

FIX

FLASHLIGHT

HOLES

OWNER

RENT

SUPERVISOR
COUNSELLOR

RELIEF

152

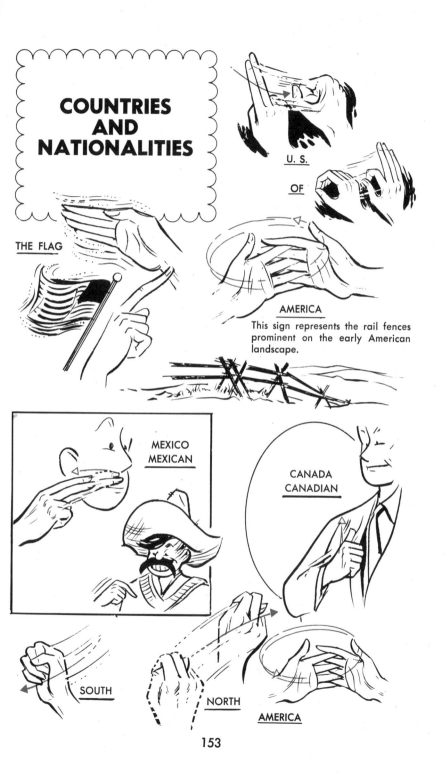

COUNTRIES AND NATIONALITIES

THE FLAG

U. S.

OF

AMERICA

This sign represents the rail fences prominent on the early American landscape.

MEXICO
MEXICAN

CANADA
CANADIAN

SOUTH

NORTH

AMERICA

153

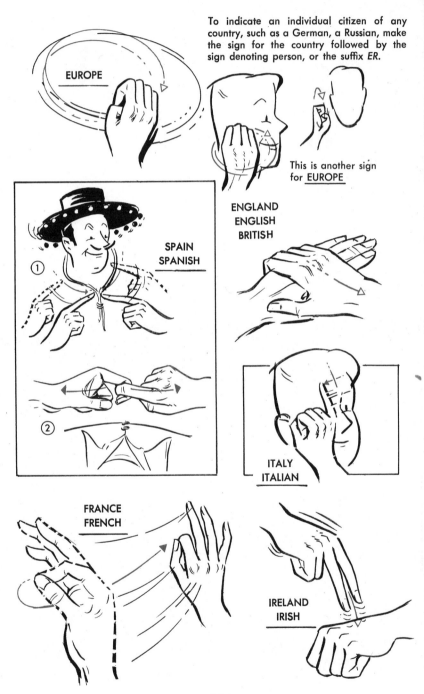

To indicate an individual citizen of any country, such as a German, a Russian, make the sign for the country followed by the sign denoting person, or the suffix ER.

EUROPE

This is another sign for EUROPE

SPAIN
SPANISH

① ②

ENGLAND
ENGLISH
BRITISH

ITALY
ITALIAN

FRANCE
FRENCH

IRELAND
IRISH

154

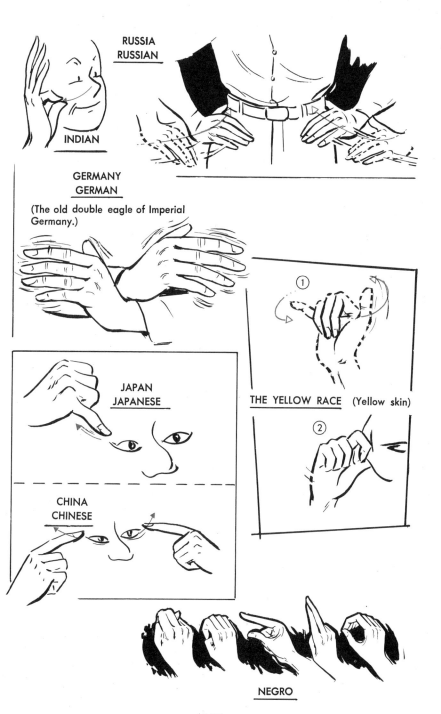

RUSSIA
RUSSIAN

INDIAN

GERMANY
GERMAN

(The old double eagle of Imperial Germany.)

THE YELLOW RACE (Yellow skin)

JAPAN
JAPANESE

CHINA
CHINESE

NEGRO

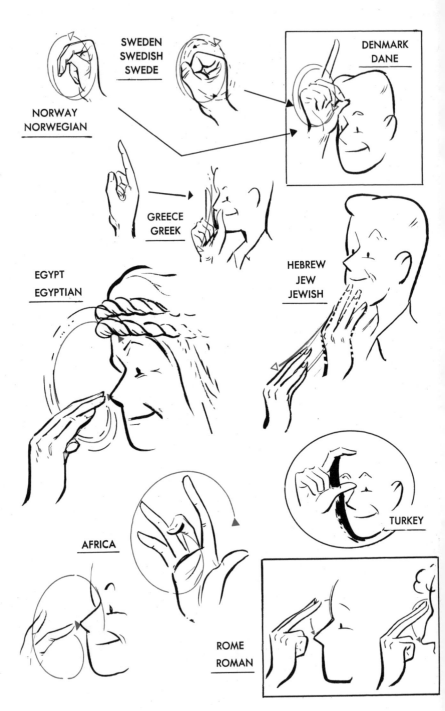

SWEDEN
SWEDISH
SWEDE

DENMARK
DANE

NORWAY
NORWEGIAN

GREECE
GREEK

EGYPT
EGYPTIAN

HEBREW
JEW
JEWISH

TURKEY

AFRICA

ROME
ROMAN

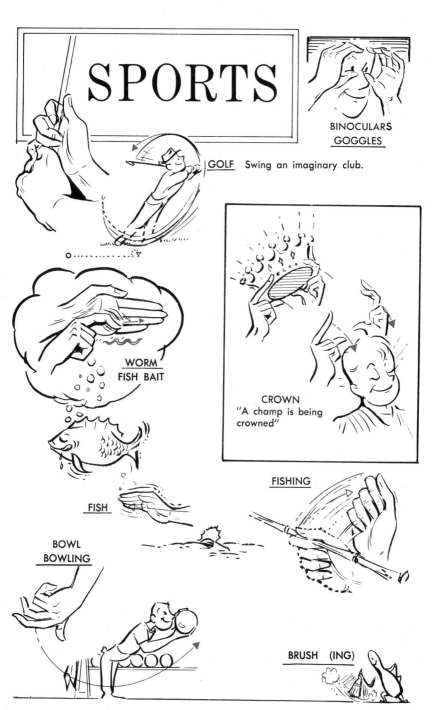

SPORTS

BINOCULARS
GOGGLES

GOLF Swing an imaginary club.

WORM
FISH BAIT

CROWN
"A champ is being crowned"

FISH

FISHING

BOWL
BOWLING

BRUSH (ING)

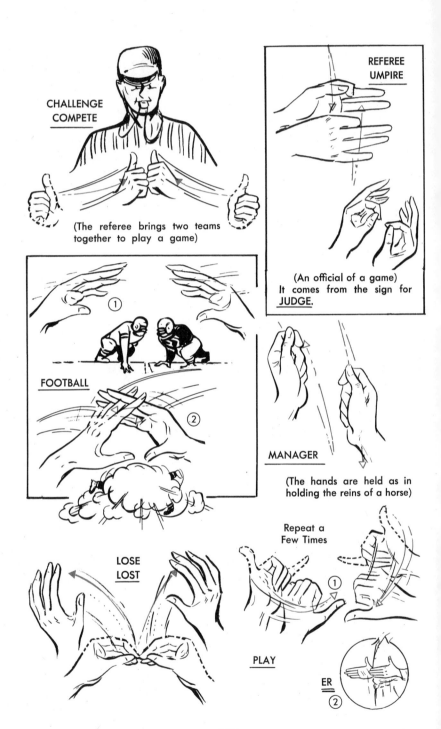

CHALLENGE
COMPETE

(The referee brings two teams
together to play a game)

REFEREE
UMPIRE

(An official of a game)
It comes from the sign for
JUDGE.

FOOTBALL

① ②

MANAGER

(The hands are held as in
holding the reins of a horse)

LOSE
LOST

Repeat a
Few Times

①

PLAY

ER
②

158

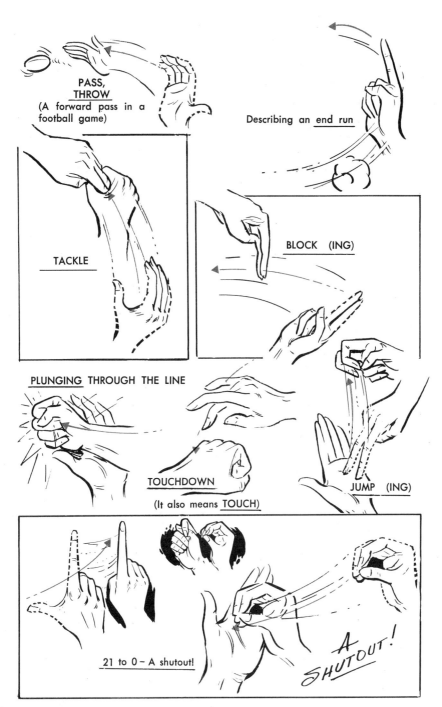

PASS,
THROW
(A forward pass in a
football game)

Describing an end run

TACKLE

BLOCK (ING)

PLUNGING THROUGH THE LINE

TOUCHDOWN

(It also means TOUCH)

JUMP (ING)

21 to 0 – A shutout!

A SHUTOUT!

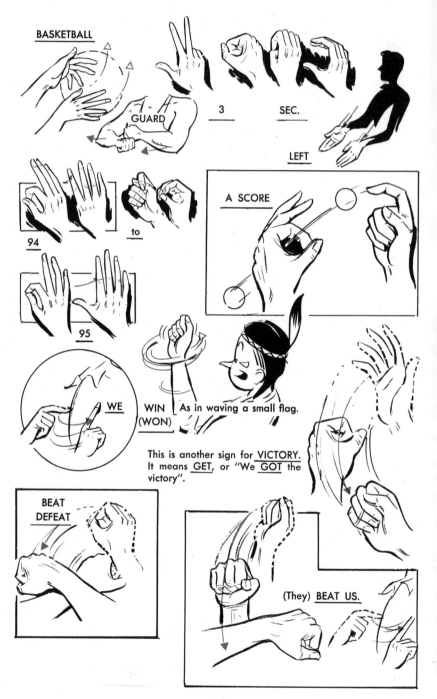

BASKETBALL

GUARD

3 SEC.

LEFT

A SCORE

94

to

95

WE

WIN (WON)

As in waving a small flag.

This is another sign for VICTORY. It means GET, or "We GOT the victory".

BEAT DEFEAT

(They) BEAT US.

160

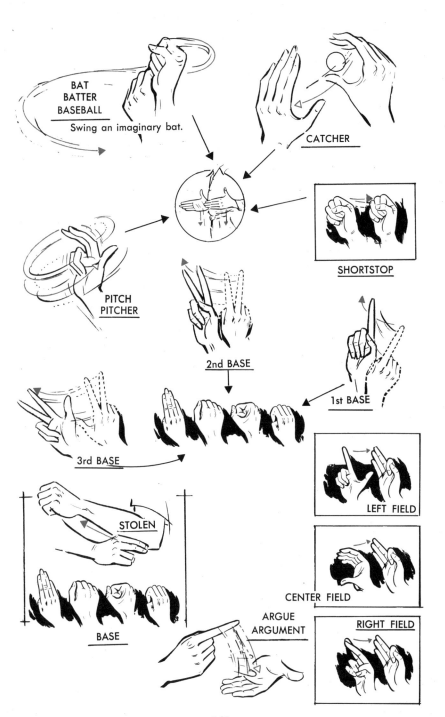

BAT
BATTER
BASEBALL

Swing an imaginary bat.

CATCHER

PITCH
PITCHER

SHORTSTOP

2nd BASE

1st BASE

3rd BASE

STOLEN

LEFT FIELD

CENTER FIELD

BASE

ARGUE
ARGUMENT

RIGHT FIELD

161

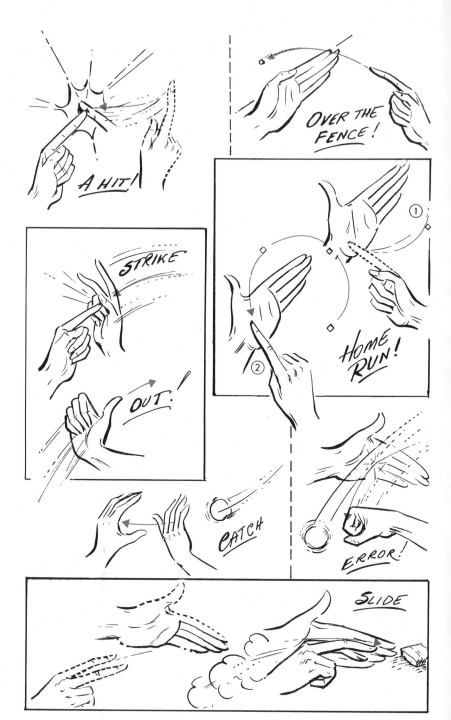

A HIT!

OVER THE FENCE!

STRIKE

OUT!

HOME RUN!

CATCH

ERROR!

SLIDE

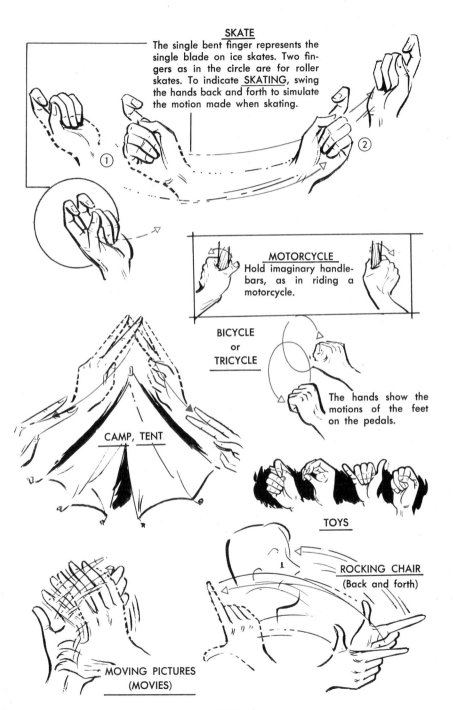

SKATE

The single bent finger represents the single blade on ice skates. Two fingers as in the circle are for roller skates. To indicate SKATING, swing the hands back and forth to simulate the motion made when skating.

① ②

MOTORCYCLE

Hold imaginary handlebars, as in riding a motorcycle.

BICYCLE
or
TRICYCLE

The hands show the motions of the feet on the pedals.

CAMP, TENT

TOYS

ROCKING CHAIR
(Back and forth)

MOVING PICTURES
(MOVIES)

163

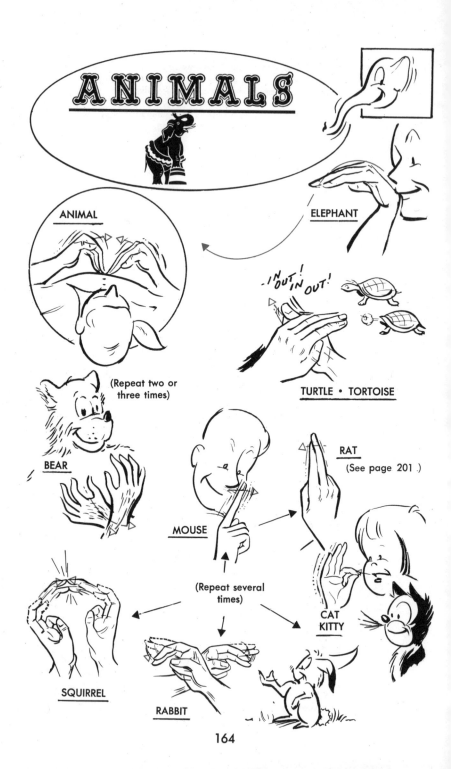

ANIMALS

ANIMAL

ELEPHANT

(Repeat two or three times)

IN OUT! IN OUT!

TURTLE • TORTOISE

BEAR

MOUSE

RAT
(See page 201.)

CAT
KITTY

(Repeat several times)

SQUIRREL

RABBIT

164

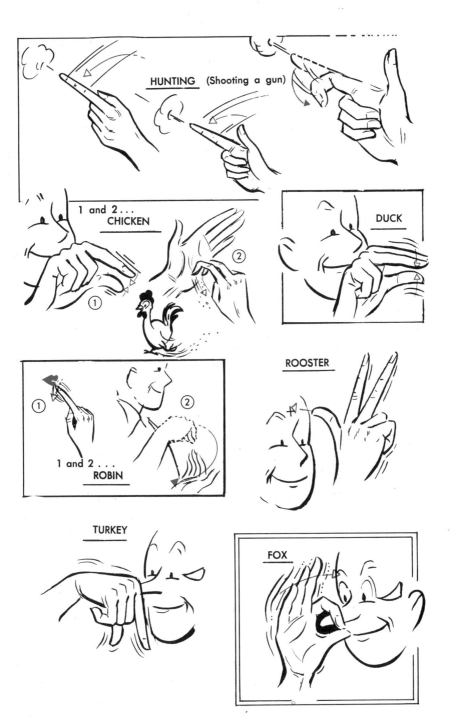

HUNTING (Shooting a gun)

1 and 2...
CHICKEN

DUCK

1 and 2...
ROBIN

ROOSTER

TURKEY

FOX

165

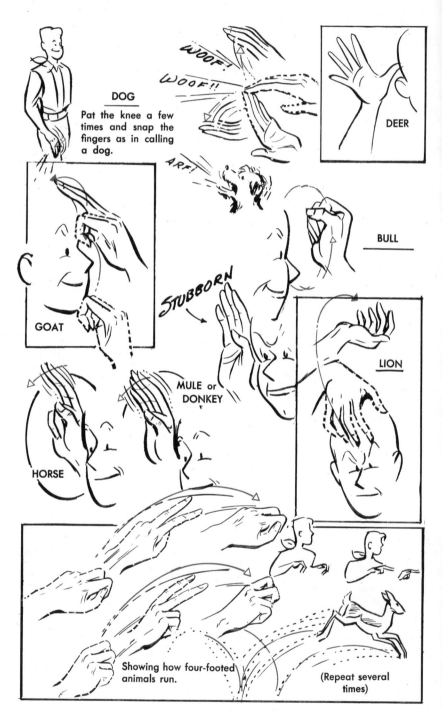

DOG

Pat the knee a few times and snap the fingers as in calling a dog.

WOOF!

WOOF!!

DEER

ARF!

BULL

GOAT

STUBBORN

LION

MULE or DONKEY

HORSE

Showing how four-footed animals run.

(Repeat several times)

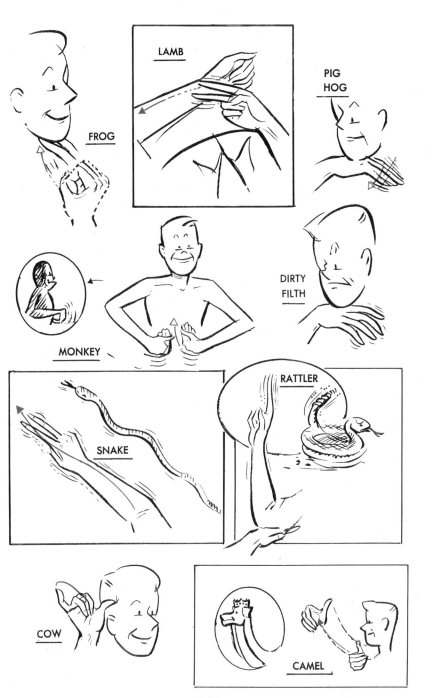

FROG

LAMB

PIG
HOG

MONKEY

DIRTY
FILTH

SNAKE

RATTLER

COW

CAMEL

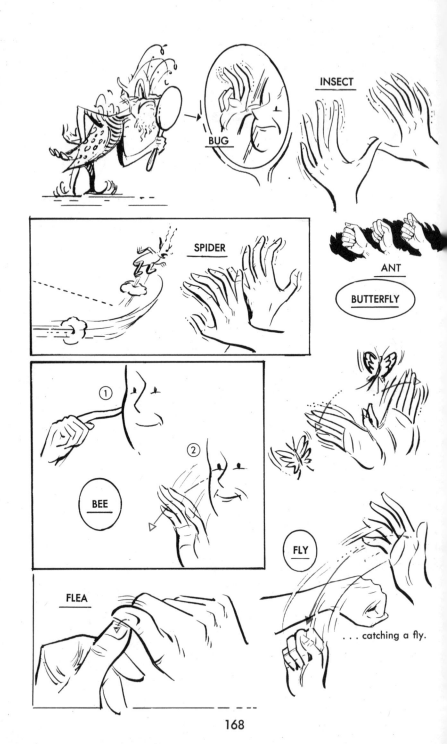

INSECT

BUG

SPIDER

ANT

BUTTERFLY

① ②

BEE

FLY

FLEA

. . . catching a fly.

168

MISCELLANEOUS

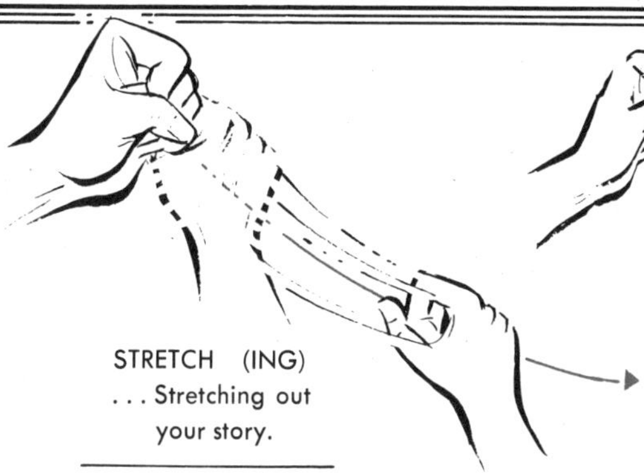

STRETCH (ING)
... Stretching out
your story.

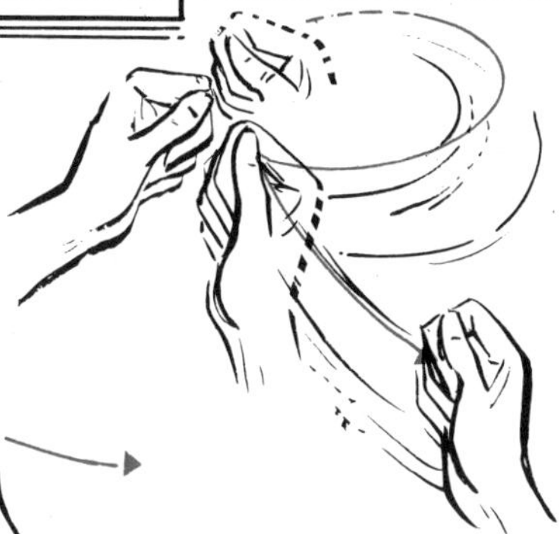

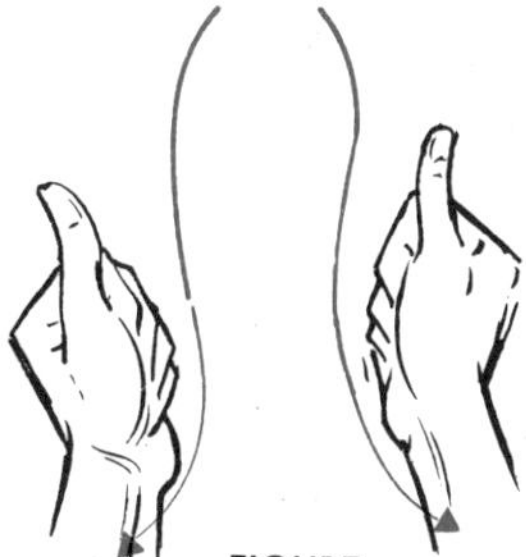

FIGURE
IDOL

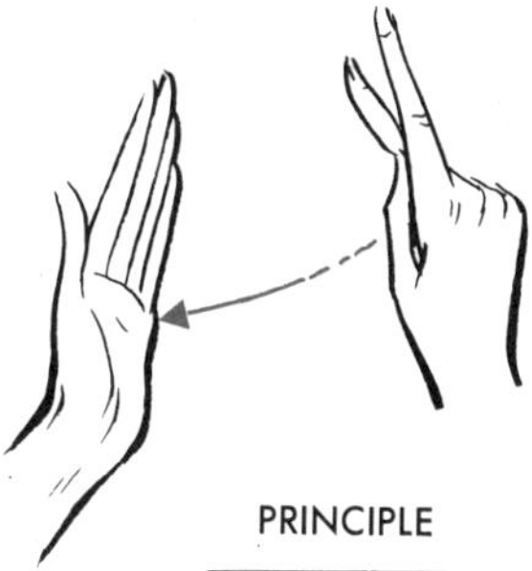

PRINCIPLE

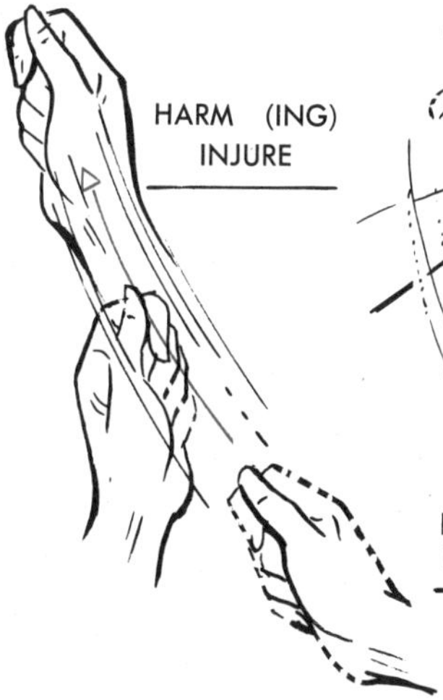

HARM (ING)
INJURE

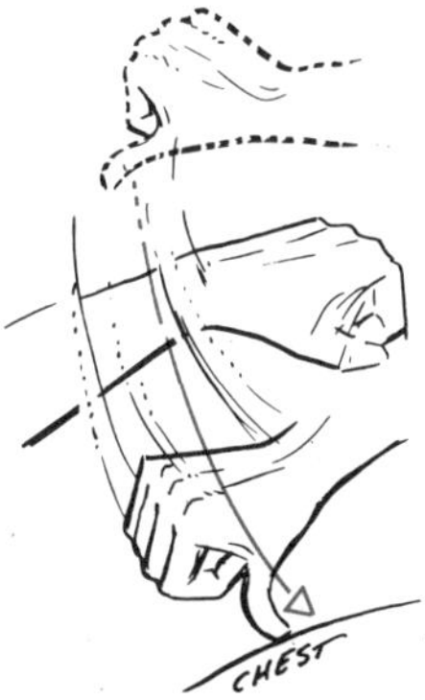

CHEST

INJURING
HARMING TOWARD SELF

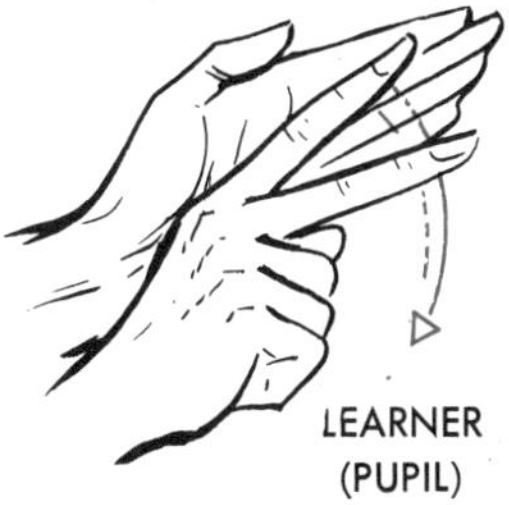

LEARNER
(PUPIL)

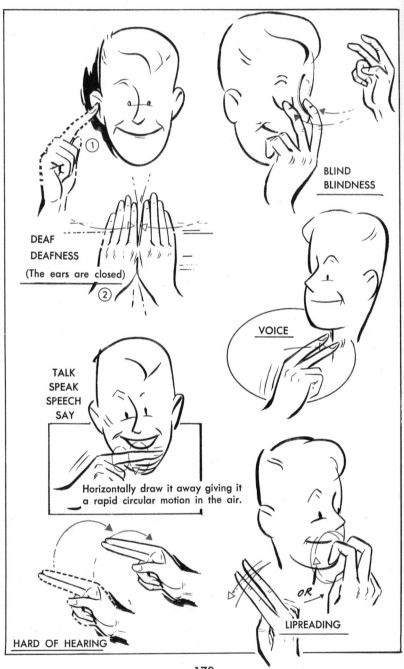

DEAF
DEAFNESS
(The ears are closed)

BLIND
BLINDNESS

VOICE

TALK
SPEAK
SPEECH
SAY

Horizontally draw it away giving it a rapid circular motion in the air.

HARD OF HEARING

LIPREADING

OR

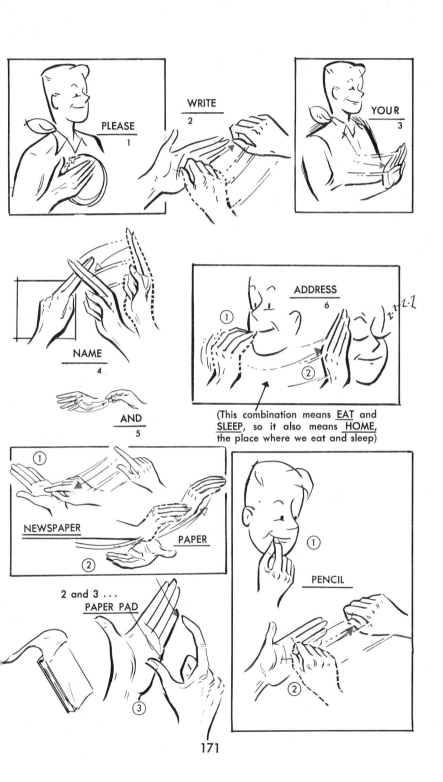

PLEASE
1

WRITE
2

YOUR
3

NAME
4

AND
5

ADDRESS
6

① ②

(This combination means <u>EAT</u> and <u>SLEEP</u>, so it also means <u>HOME</u>, the place where we eat and sleep)

NEWSPAPER
①
②

PAPER

2 and 3 . . .
PAPER PAD
③

PENCIL
①
②

171

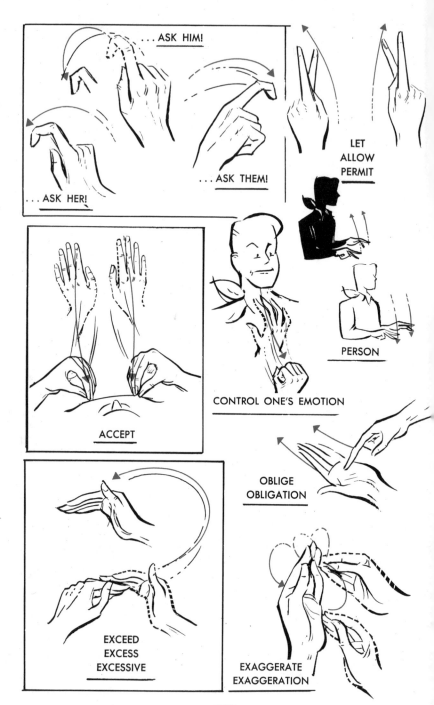

... ASK HIM!

... ASK THEM!

... ASK HER!

LET
ALLOW
PERMIT

PERSON

CONTROL ONE'S EMOTION

ACCEPT

OBLIGE
OBLIGATION

EXCEED
EXCESS
EXCESSIVE

EXAGGERATE
EXAGGERATION

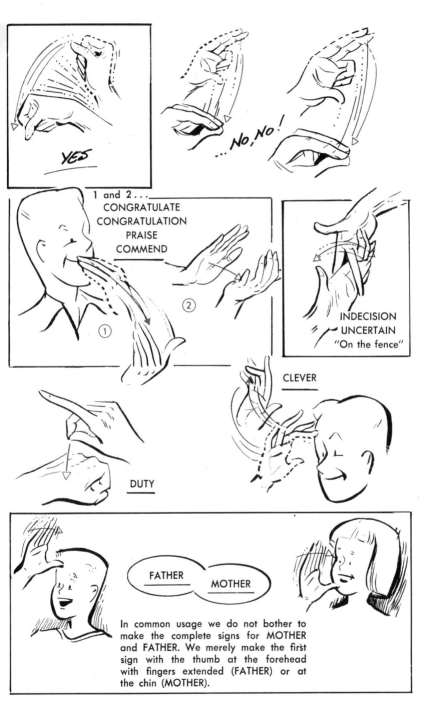

YES

...No, No!

1 and 2...
CONGRATULATE
CONGRATULATION
PRAISE
COMMEND

①
②

INDECISION
UNCERTAIN
"On the fence"

CLEVER

DUTY

FATHER — MOTHER

In common usage we do not bother to make the complete signs for MOTHER and FATHER. We merely make the first sign with the thumb at the forehead with fingers extended (FATHER) or at the chin (MOTHER).

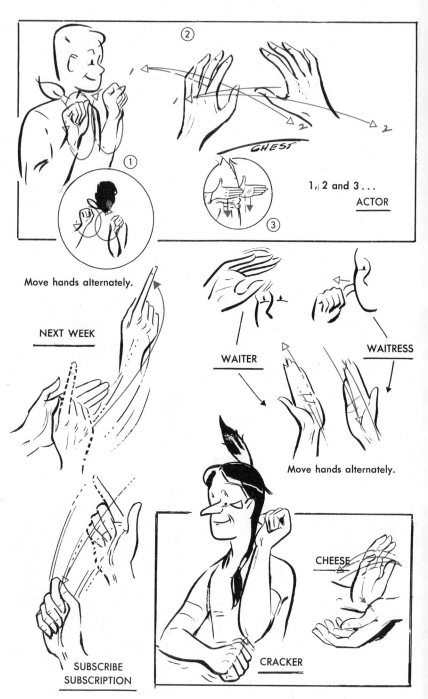

② CHEST

1, 2 and 3 . . .
ACTOR

① Move hands alternately.

③

NEXT WEEK

WAITER

WAITRESS

Move hands alternately.

SUBSCRIBE
SUBSCRIPTION

CHEESE

CRACKER

174

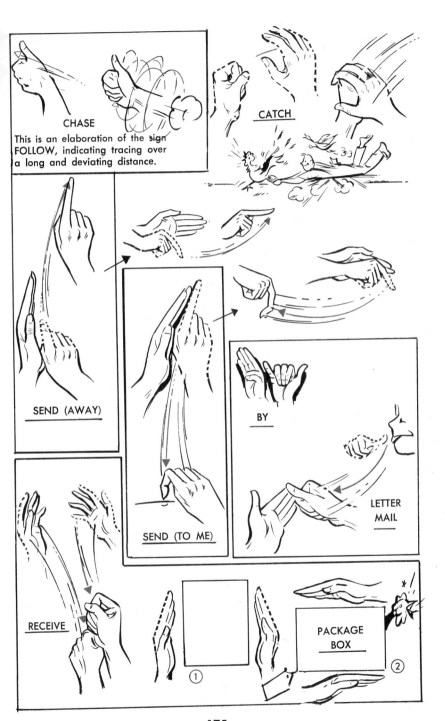

CHASE

This is an elaboration of the sign FOLLOW, indicating tracing over a long and deviating distance.

CATCH

SEND (AWAY)

SEND (TO ME)

BY

LETTER MAIL

RECEIVE

① PACKAGE BOX ②

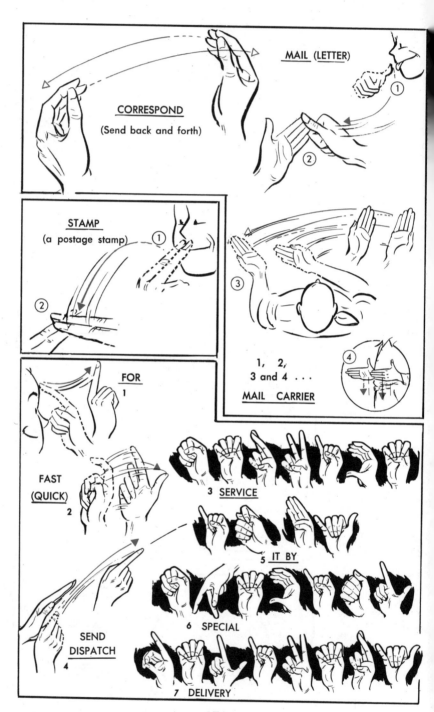

MAIL (LETTER)

CORRESPOND
(Send back and forth)

STAMP
(a postage stamp)

1, 2,
3 and 4 . . .
MAIL CARRIER

FOR
1

FAST
(QUICK)
2

3 SERVICE

5 IT BY

6 SPECIAL

SEND
DISPATCH
4

7 DELIVERY

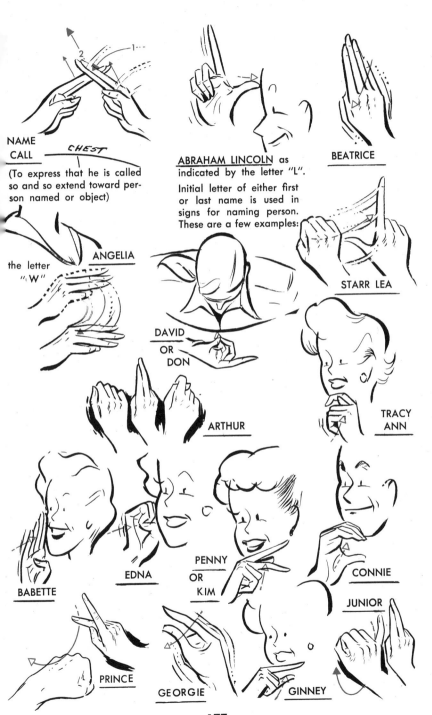

NAME CALL *CHEST*

(To express that he is called so and so extend toward person named or object)

ABRAHAM LINCOLN as indicated by the letter "L".

Initial letter of either first or last name is used in signs for naming person. These are a few examples:

BEATRICE

the letter "W"

ANGELIA

STARR LEA

DAVID OR DON

TRACY ANN

ARTHUR

BABETTE

EDNA

PENNY OR KIM

CONNIE

JUNIOR

PRINCE

GEORGIE

GINNEY

177

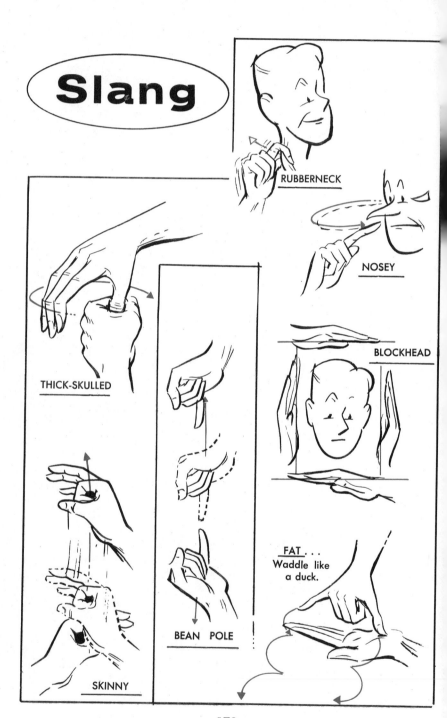

Slang

RUBBERNECK

NOSEY

THICK-SKULLED

BLOCKHEAD

BEAN POLE

SKINNY

FAT . . .
Waddle like
a duck.

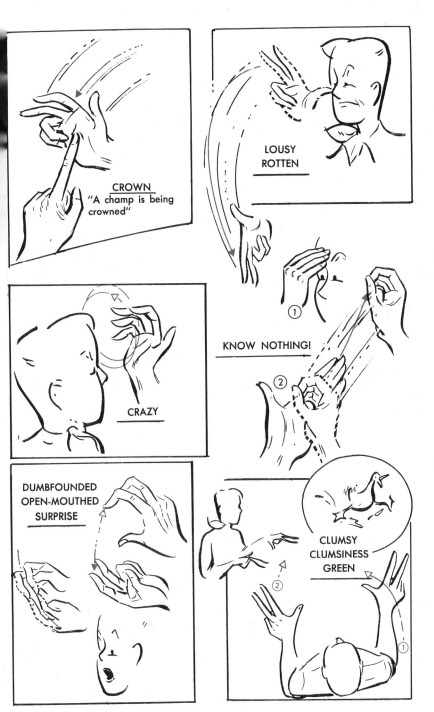

CROWN
"A champ is being crowned"

LOUSY
ROTTEN

CRAZY

KNOW NOTHING!

DUMBFOUNDED
OPEN-MOUTHED
SURPRISE

CLUMSY
CLUMSINESS
GREEN

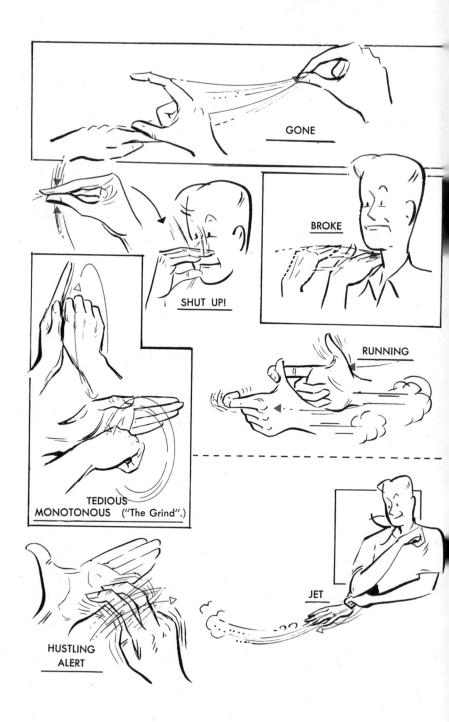

GONE

BROKE

SHUT UP!

RUNNING

TEDIOUS
MONOTONOUS ("The Grind".)

JET

HUSTLING
ALERT

180

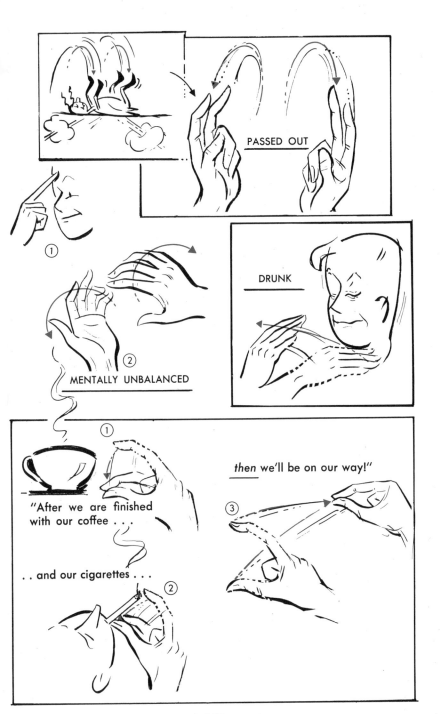

PASSED OUT

DRUNK

MENTALLY UNBALANCED

"After we are finished
with our coffee . . .

. . and our cigarettes . . .

then we'll be on our way!"

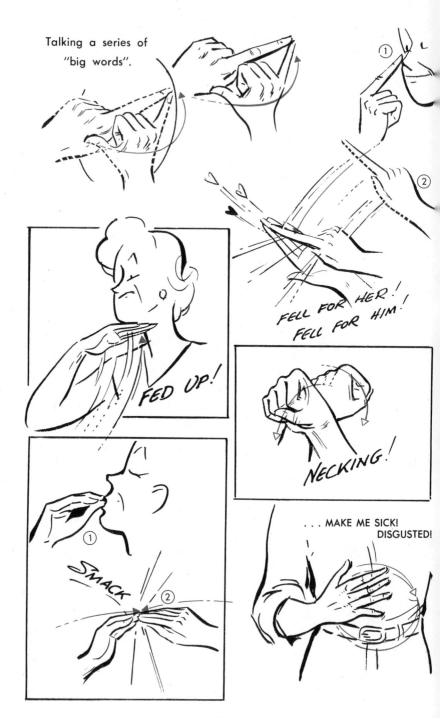

Talking a series of "big words".

FED UP!

FELL FOR HER!
FELL FOR HIM!

NECKING!

SMACK

... MAKE ME SICK!
DISGUSTED!

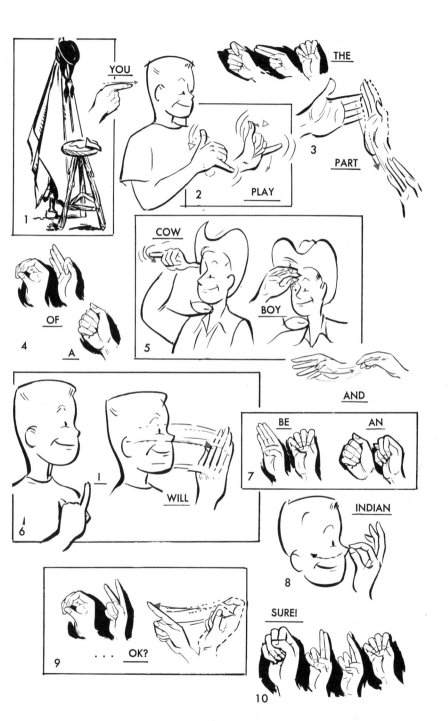

YOU

2 PLAY

3 THE PART

4 OF A

5 COW BOY

AND

6 I WILL

7 BE AN

8 INDIAN

9 . . . OK?

SURE!

10

183

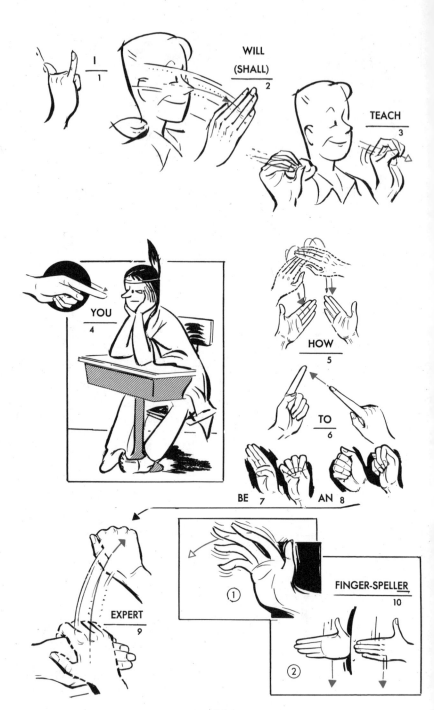

WILL (SHALL)

TEACH

YOU

HOW

TO

BE

AN

EXPERT

FINGER-SPELLER

184

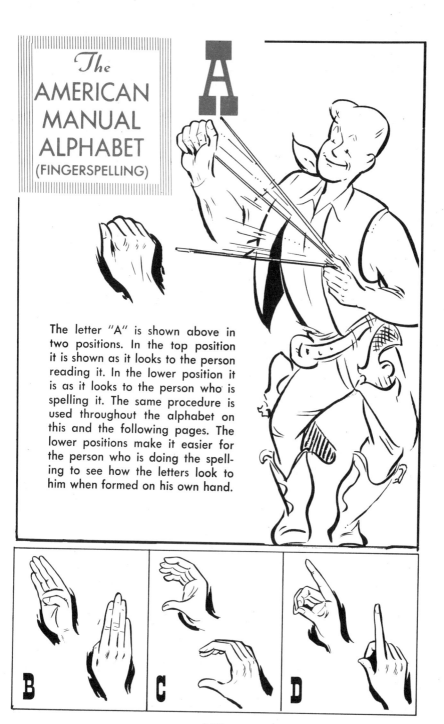

The AMERICAN MANUAL ALPHABET
(FINGERSPELLING)

The letter "A" is shown above in two positions. In the top position it is shown as it looks to the person reading it. In the lower position it is as it looks to the person who is spelling it. The same procedure is used throughout the alphabet on this and the following pages. The lower positions make it easier for the person who is doing the spelling to see how the letters look to him when formed on his own hand.

B

C

D

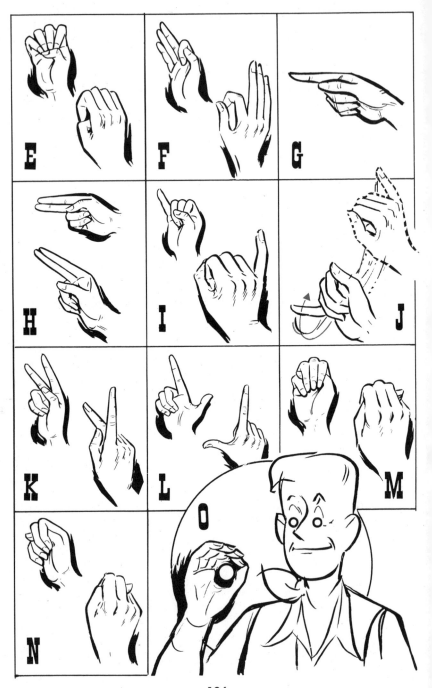

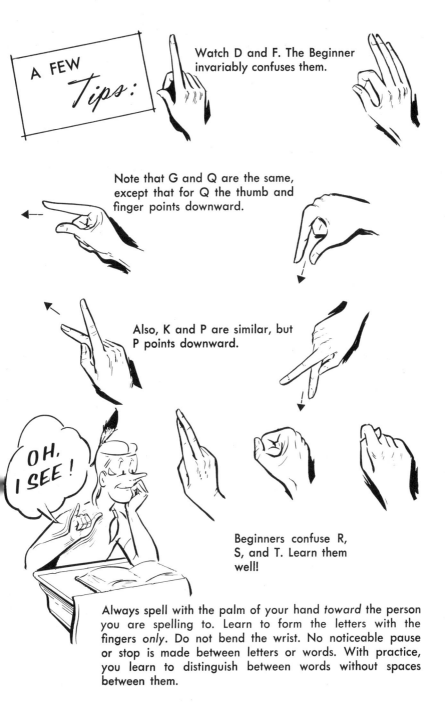

A FEW *Tips:*

Watch D and F. The Beginner invariably confuses them.

Note that G and Q are the same, except that for Q the thumb and finger points downward.

Also, K and P are similar, but P points downward.

OH, I SEE!

Beginners confuse R, S, and T. Learn them well!

Always spell with the palm of your hand *toward* the person you are spelling to. Learn to form the letters with the fingers *only*. Do not bend the wrist. No noticeable pause or stop is made between letters or words. With practice, you learn to distinguish between words without spaces between them.

187

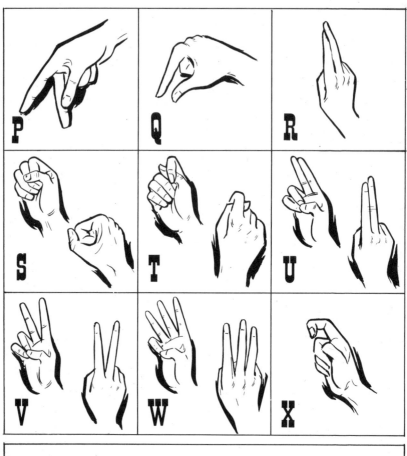

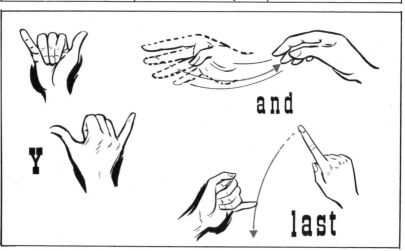

188

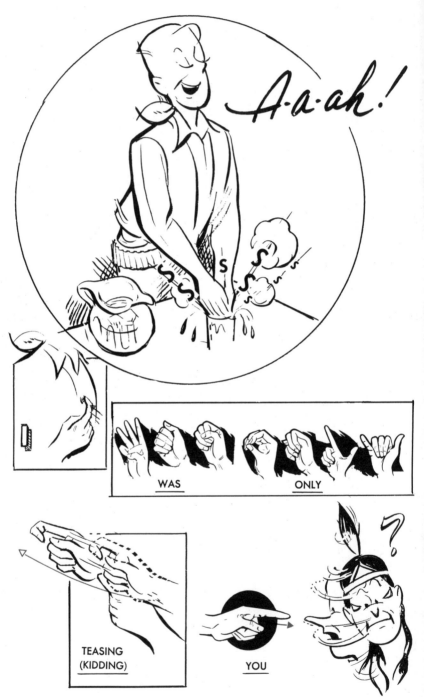

A·a·ah!

WAS   ONLY

TEASING
(KIDDING)

YOU

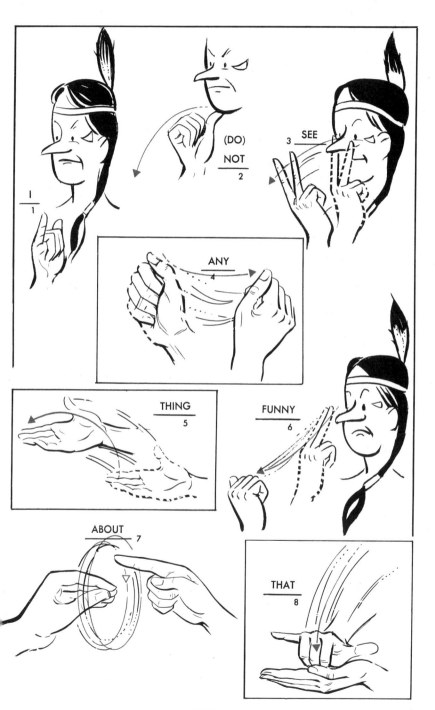

1/1

(DO)
NOT
2

3 SEE

ANY
4

THING
5

FUNNY
6

ABOUT
7

THAT
8

191

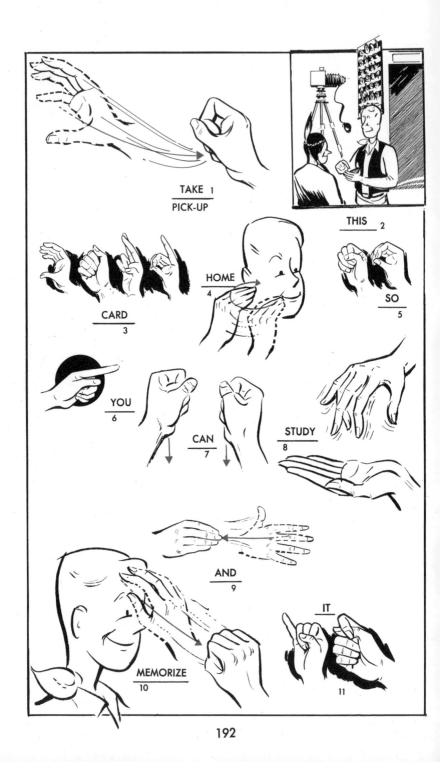

TAKE 1
PICK-UP

THIS 2

CARD 3

HOME 4

SO 5

YOU 6

CAN 7

STUDY 8

AND 9

MEMORIZE 10

IT 11

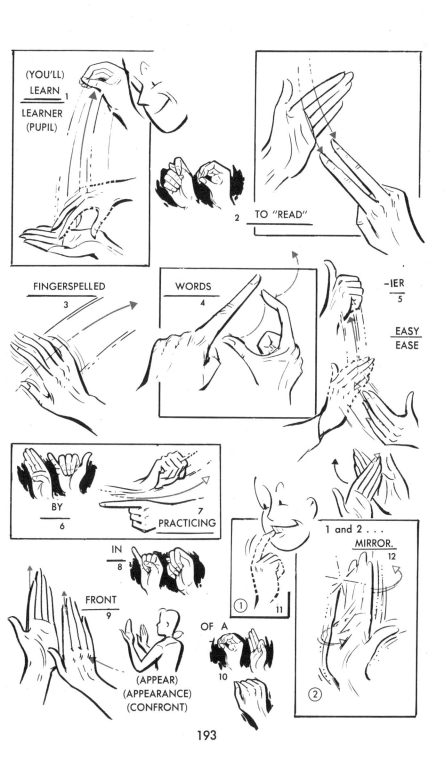

(YOU'LL)
LEARN
LEARNER
(PUPIL)
1

TO "READ"
2

FINGERSPELLED
3

WORDS
4

-IER
5

EASY
EASE

BY
6

PRACTICING
7

IN
8

1 and 2 . . .
MIRROR.
12

FRONT
9

(APPEAR)
(APPEARANCE)
(CONFRONT)

OF A
10

11

193

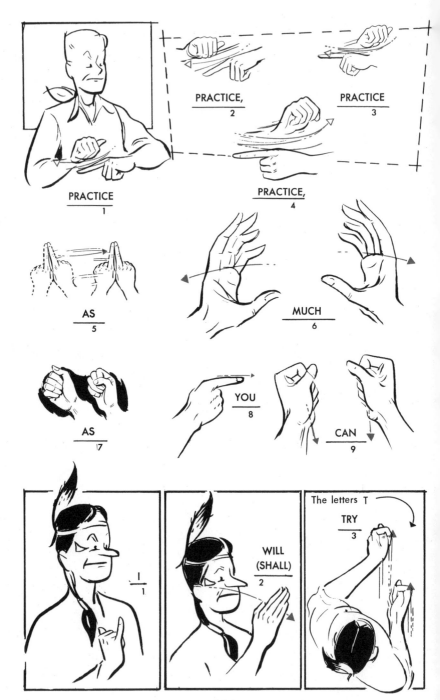

PRACTICE
1

PRACTICE,
2

PRACTICE
3

PRACTICE,
4

AS
5

MUCH
6

AS
7

YOU
8

CAN
9

1
1

WILL
(SHALL)
2

The letters T
TRY
3

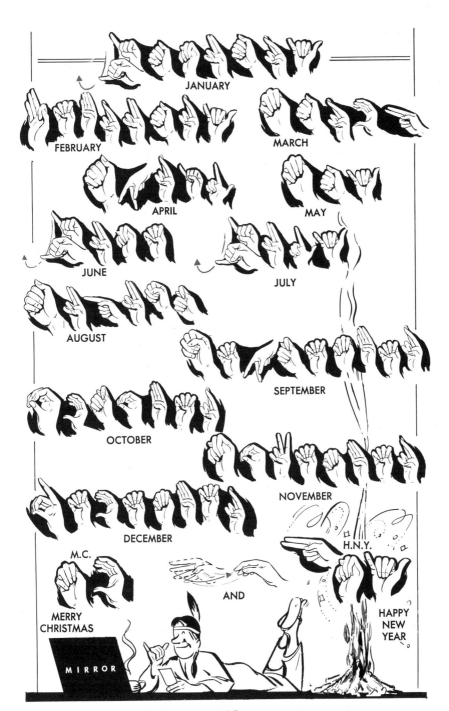

JANUARY

FEBRUARY

MARCH

APRIL

MAY

JUNE

JULY

AUGUST

SEPTEMBER

OCTOBER

NOVEMBER

DECEMBER

H.N.Y.

M.C.

AND

MERRY CHRISTMAS

MIRROR

HAPPY NEW YEAR

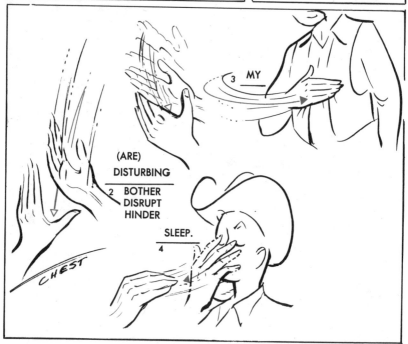

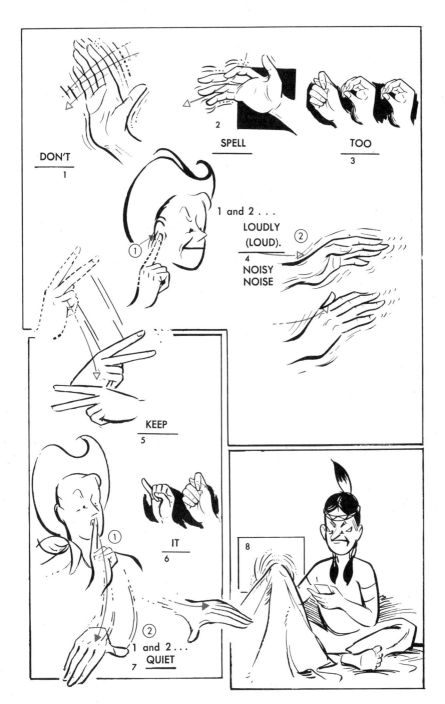

DON'T
1

SPELL
2

TOO
3

1 and 2 . . .
LOUDLY
(LOUD).
4
NOISY
NOISE

KEEP
5

IT
6

1 and 2 . . .
QUIET
7

8

197

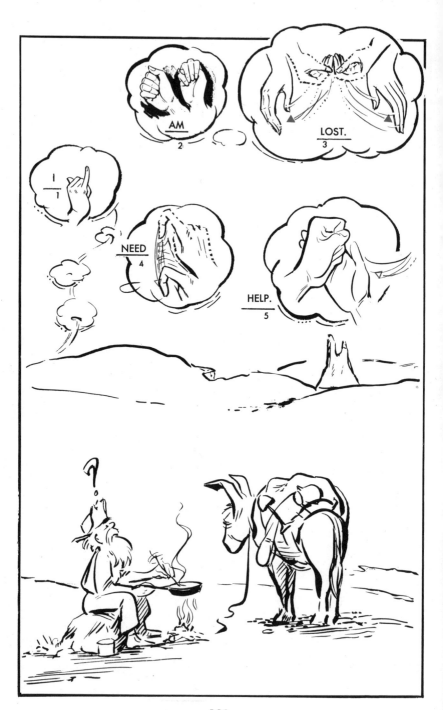

TROUBLE?

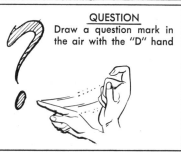

QUESTION
Draw a question mark in
the air with the "D" hand

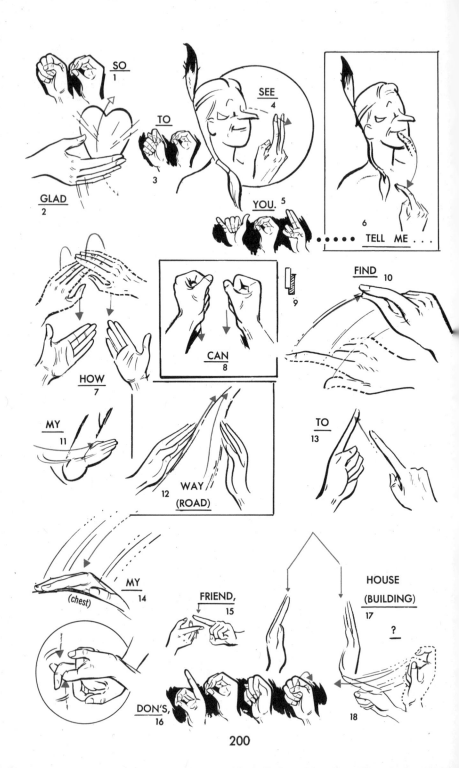

SO
1

GLAD
2

TO
3

SEE
4

YOU.
5

6

• • • • • TELL ME . . .

HOW
7

CAN
8

9

FIND
10

MY
11

WAY
(ROAD)
12

TO
13

MY
(chest)
14

FRIEND,
15

HOUSE
(BUILDING)
17

?

DON'S,
16

18

200

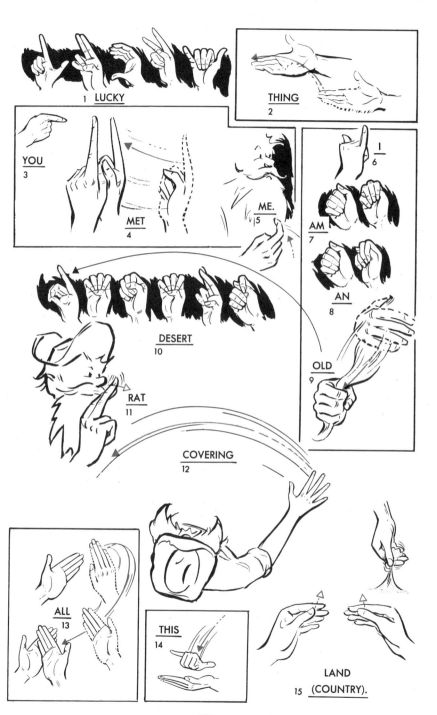

1 LUCKY

THING
2

YOU
3

MET
4

ME.
5

I
6

AM
7

AN
8

OLD
9

DESERT
10

RAT
11

COVERING
12

ALL
13

THIS
14

LAND
15 (COUNTRY).

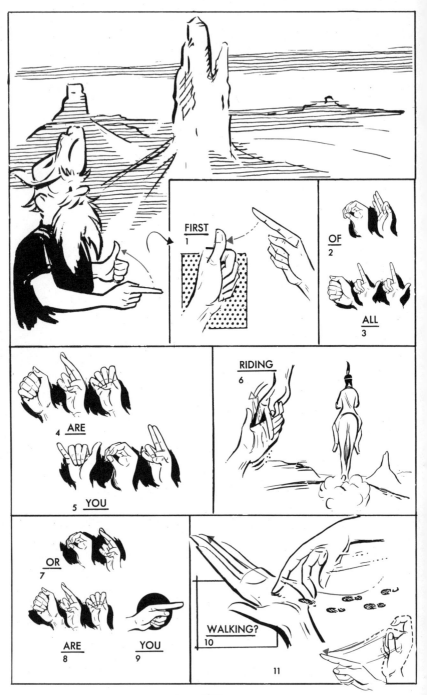

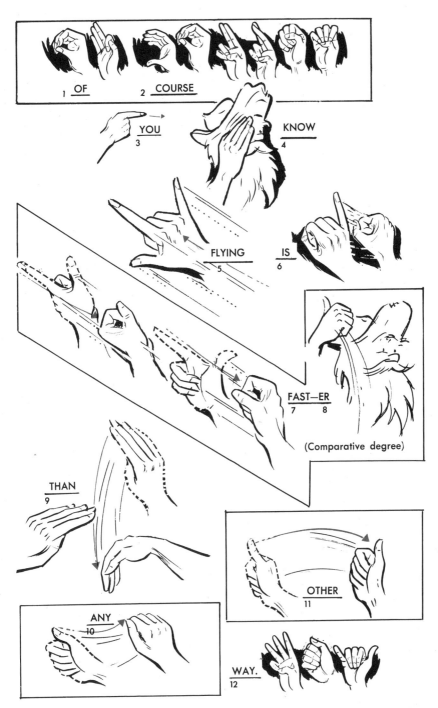

1 OF 2 COURSE

3 YOU

KNOW 4

FLYING 5 IS 6

FAST—ER 7 8

(Comparative degree)

THAN 9

OTHER 11

ANY 10

WAY. 12

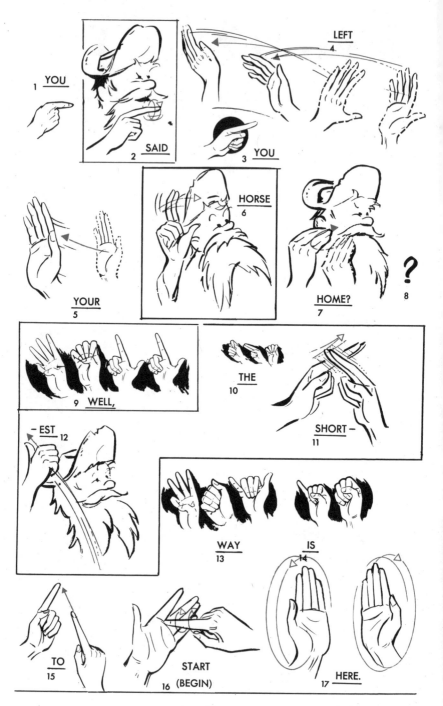

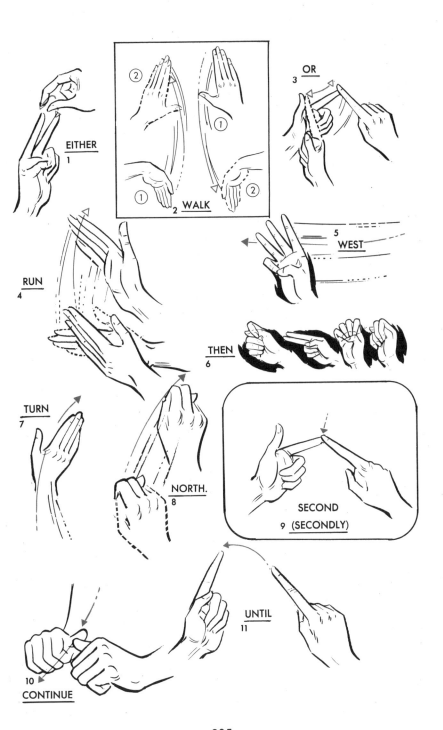

EITHER
1

WALK
2

OR
3

RUN
4

WEST
5

THEN
6

TURN
7

NORTH.
8

SECOND
9 (SECONDLY)

CONTINUE
10

UNTIL
11

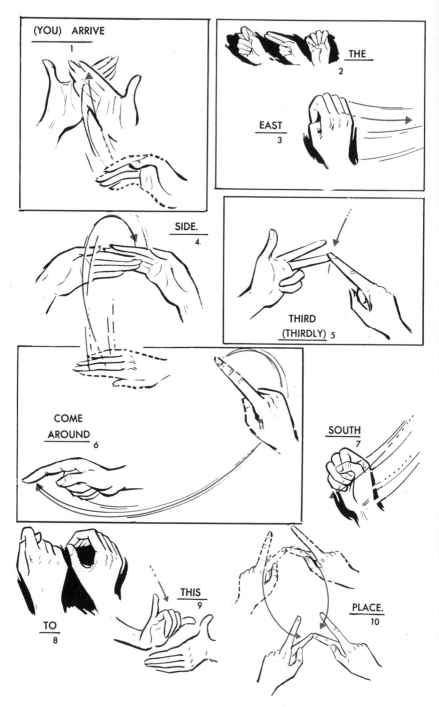

(YOU) ARRIVE
1

THE
2

EAST
3

SIDE.
4.

THIRD
(THIRDLY) 5

COME
AROUND
6

SOUTH
7

TO
8

THIS
9

PLACE.
10

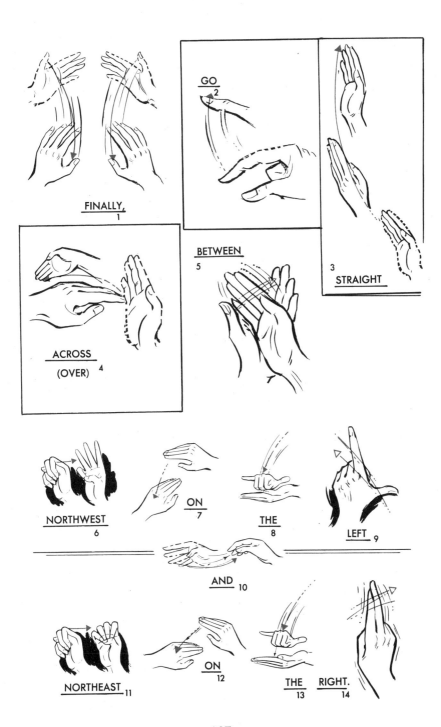

FINALLY,
1

GO
2

STRAIGHT
3

ACROSS
(OVER) 4

BETWEEN
5

NORTHWEST
6

ON
7

THE
8

LEFT 9

AND 10

NORTHEAST
11

ON
12

THE
13

RIGHT.
14

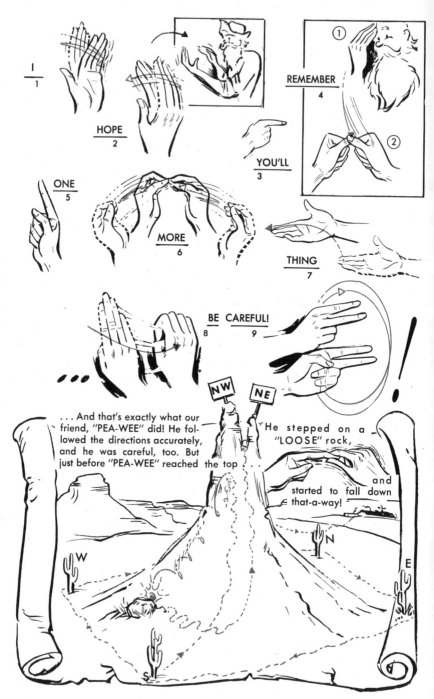

HOPE
2

1/1

REMEMBER
4

YOU'LL
3

ONE
5

MORE
6

THING
7

BE CAREFUL!
8   9

... And that's exactly what our friend, "PEA-WEE" did! He followed the directions accurately, and he was careful, too. But just before "PEA-WEE" reached the top ...

He stepped on a "LOOSE" rock,

and started to fall down that-a-way!

208

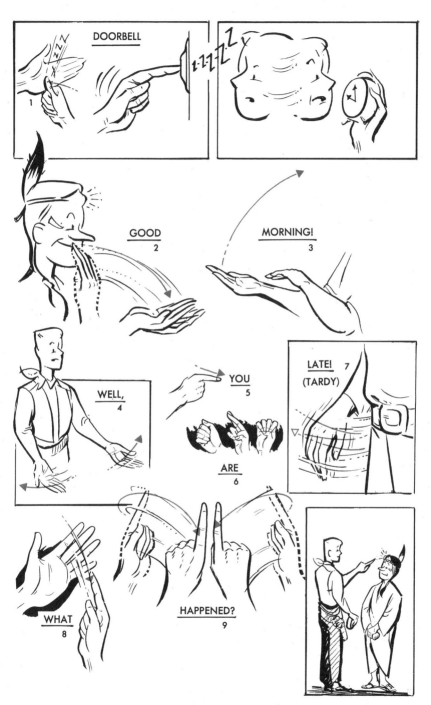

209

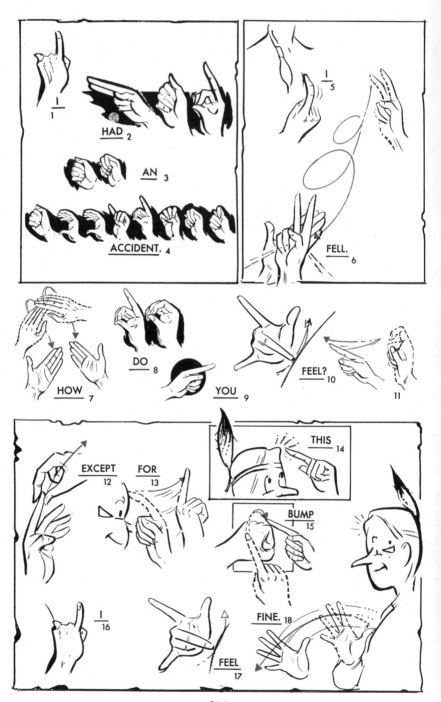

I
1

HAD 2

AN 3

ACCIDENT. 4

I
5

FELL. 6

HOW 7

DO 8

YOU 9

FEEL? 10

11

EXCEPT 12

FOR 13

THIS 14

BUMP 15

I
16

FEEL 17

FINE. 18

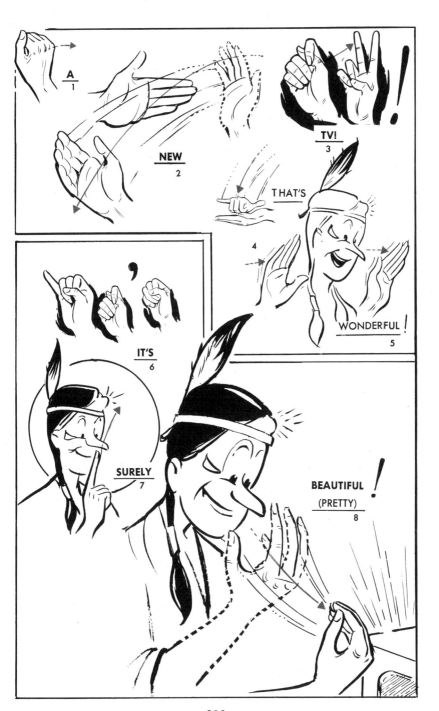

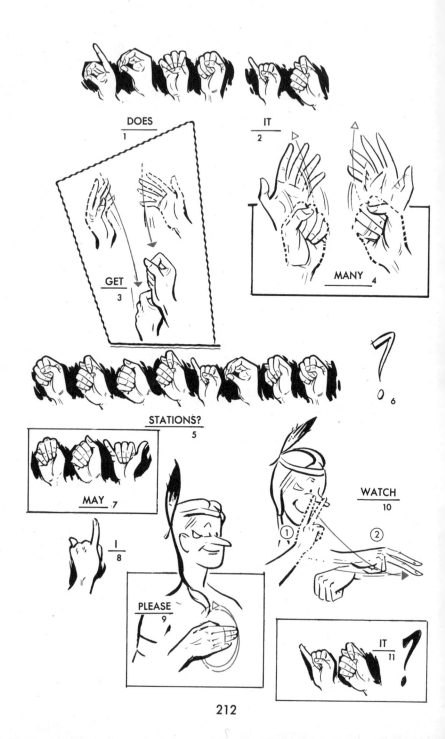

DOES
1

IT
2

GET
3

MANY
4

STATIONS?
5

$\dfrac{}{}$ 6

MAY
7

I
8

PLEASE
9

WATCH
10

① ②

IT
11

212

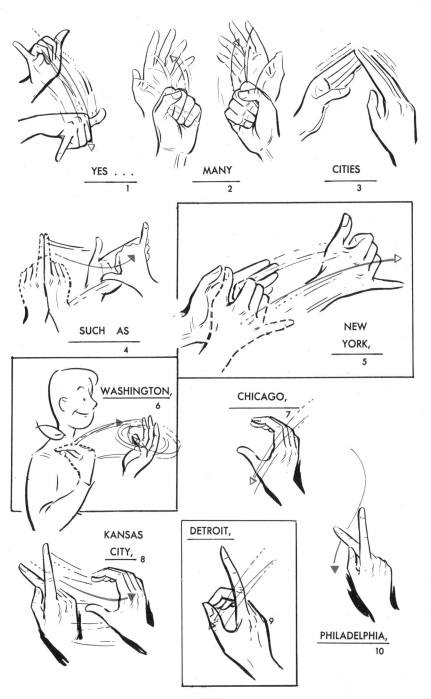

YES . . .
1

MANY
2

CITIES
3

SUCH AS
4

NEW YORK,
5

WASHINGTON,
6

CHICAGO,
7

KANSAS CITY,
8

DETROIT,
9

PHILADELPHIA,
10

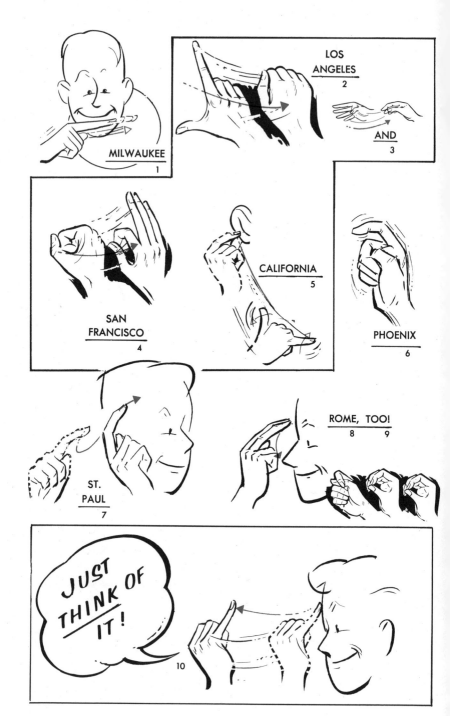

MILWAUKEE
1

LOS ANGELES
2

AND
3

SAN FRANCISCO
4

CALIFORNIA
5

PHOENIX
6

ST. PAUL
7

ROME, TOO!
8   9

JUST THINK OF IT!
10

214

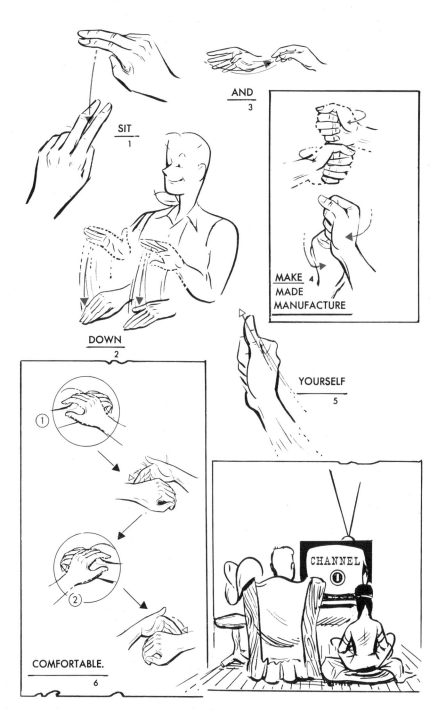

SIT
1

AND
3

DOWN
2

MAKE 4
MADE
MANUFACTURE

YOURSELF
5

CHANNEL

COMFORTABLE.
6

215

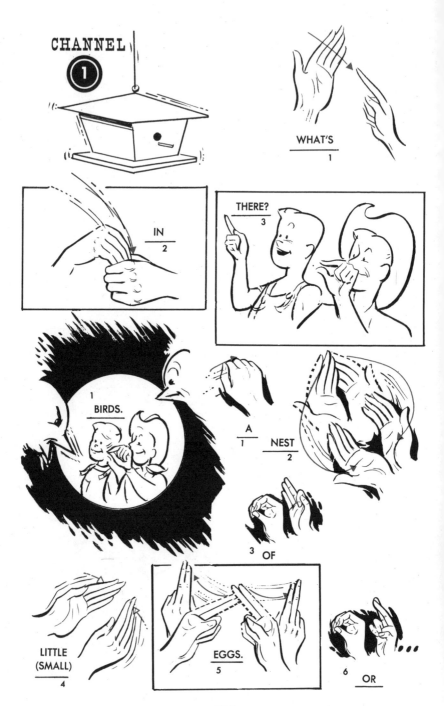

CHANNEL 1

WHAT'S
1

IN
2

THERE?
3

BIRDS.
1

A
1

NEST
2

3 OF

LITTLE
(SMALL)
4

EGGS.
5

6 OR

216

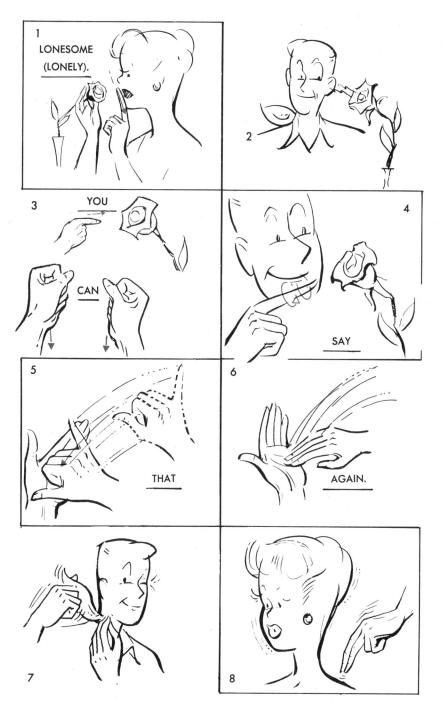

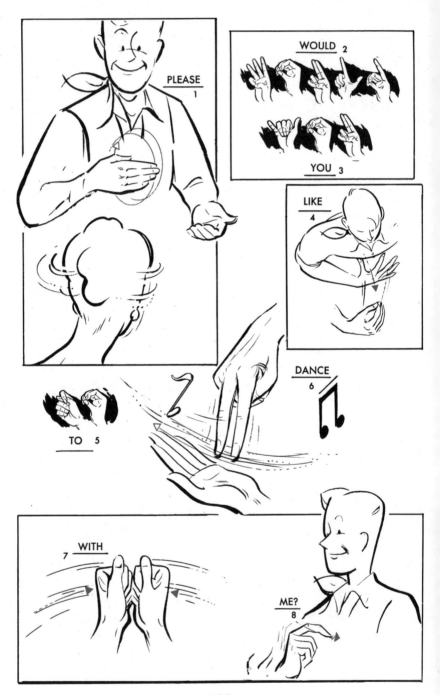

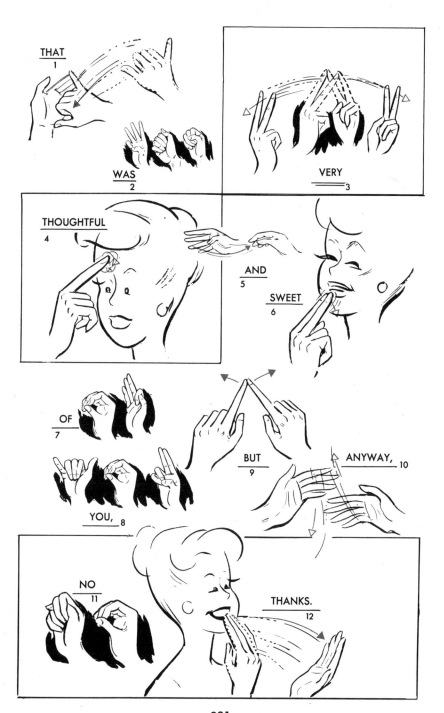

THAT
1

WAS
2

VERY
3

THOUGHTFUL
4

AND
5

SWEET
6

OF
7

YOU,
8

BUT
9

ANYWAY,
10

NO
11

THANKS.
12

221

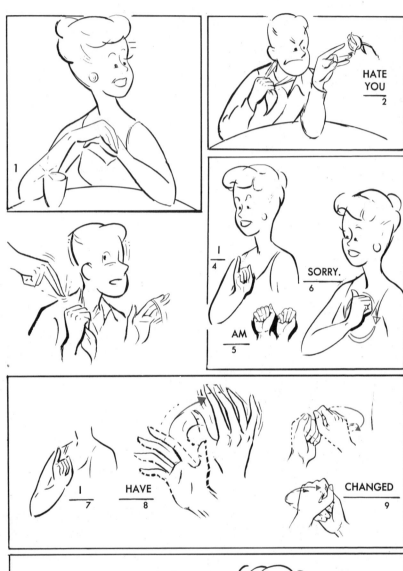

HATE YOU
2

I
4

SORRY.
6

AM
5

I
7

HAVE
8

CHANGED
9

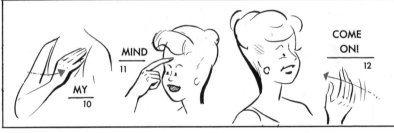

MY
10

MIND
11

COME ON!
12

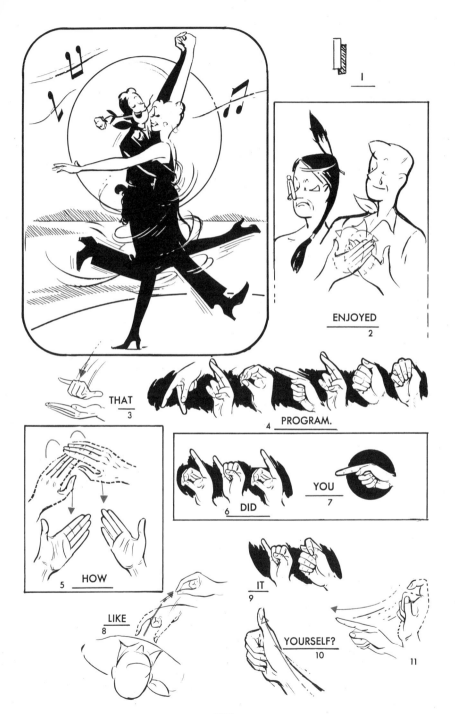

ENJOYED
2

THAT
3

PROGRAM.
4

HOW
5

DID
6

YOU
7

LIKE
8

IT
9

YOURSELF?
10

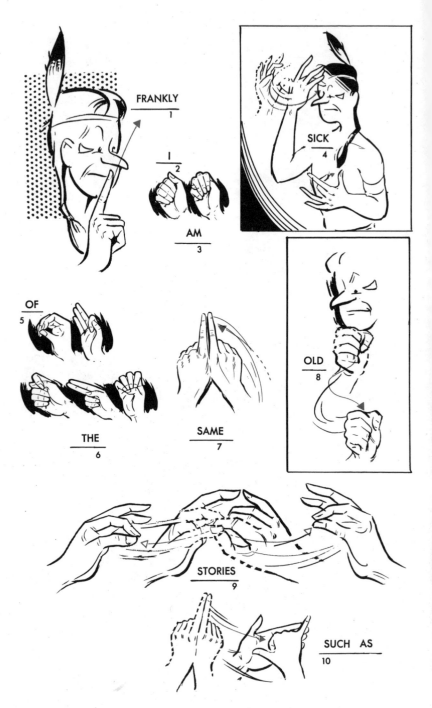

FRANKLY
1

I
2

AM
3

SICK
4

OF
5

THE
6

SAME
7

OLD
8

STORIES
9

SUCH AS
10

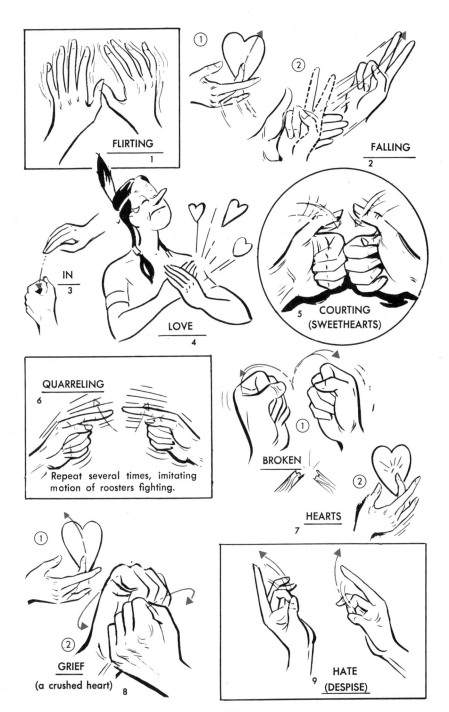

FLIRTING
1

① ② FALLING
2

IN
3

LOVE
4

5 COURTING
(SWEETHEARTS)

QUARRELING
6

Repeat several times, imitating motion of roosters fighting.

① BROKEN

② HEARTS
7

① ② GRIEF
(a crushed heart)
8

9 HATE
(DESPISE)

225

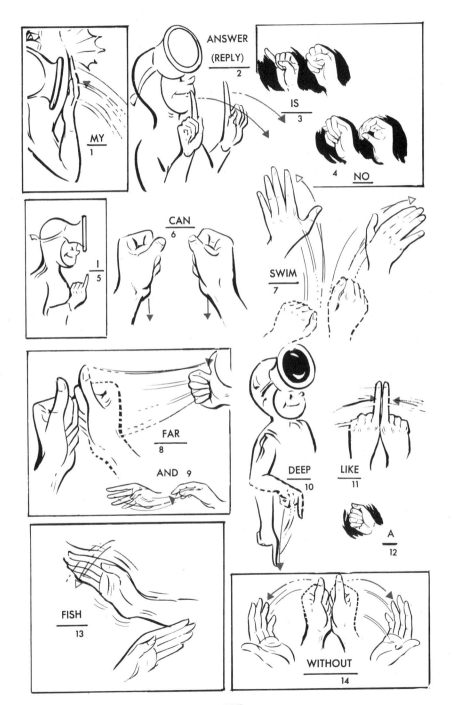

MY
1

ANSWER
(REPLY)
2

IS
3

NO
4

I
5

CAN
6

SWIM
7

FAR
8

AND 9

DEEP
10

LIKE
11

A
12

FISH
13

WITHOUT
14

227

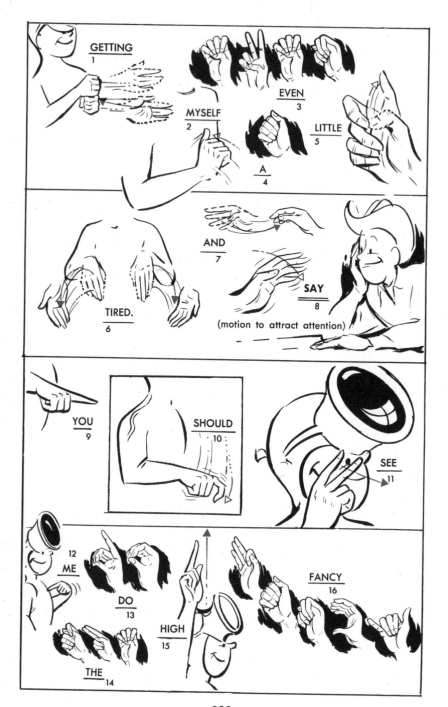

GETTING
1

MYSELF
2

EVEN
3

A
4

LITTLE
5

TIRED.
6

AND
7

SAY
8

(motion to attract attention)

YOU
9

SHOULD
10

SEE
11

ME
12

DO
13

THE
14

HIGH
15

FANCY
16

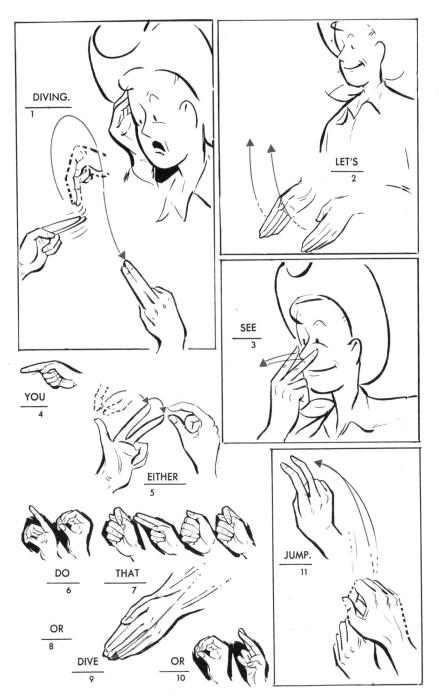

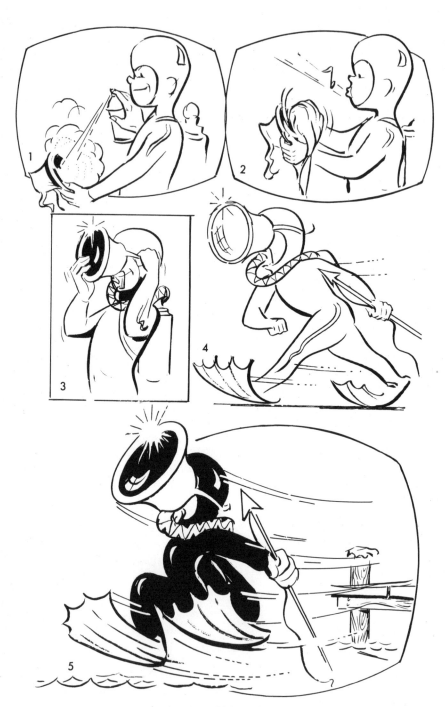

231

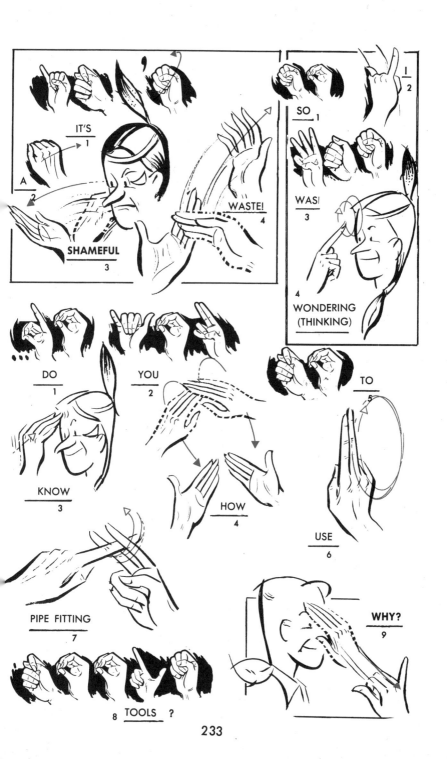

IT'S
1

A
2

SHAMEFUL
3

WASTE!
4

SO
1

I
2

WAS
3

WONDERING
(THINKING)
4

DO
1

YOU
2

KNOW
3

HOW
4

TO
5

USE
6

PIPE FITTING
7

TOOLS ?
8

WHY?
9

233

PLESE
1

(See page 107)
2

WHAT
3

"PEA-WEE"
4

5 RAISED

AND
6

IN 8

HIS
9

GARDEN 10

7
GREW

234

Index

NOTE: 1) Two or more page numbers indicate different signs
2) Page numbers in parentheses indicate repetitions of the same sign
3) * Words are fingerspelled

238

HAPPEN 58 (74, 209)
HAPPINESS 46
HAPPY 46 (79)
HAPPY NEW YEAR 79, 195
HARD 64
HARD-BOILED 60
HARD OF HEARING 170
HARDSHIP 41
HARM 169
HASTE 42
HATE 45 (222, 225)
HAVE 25 (210)
HAVE TO 25
HE 1
HEADACHE 119
HEAR 55 (150)
HEART 44 (225)
HEART ATTACK 119
HEARTBEAT 123
HEARTY 120
HEAT 101
HEAVEN 94
HEAVY 86
HEBREW 156
HEIGHT 69
HELL 98
HELP 36 (198)
HEN 165
*HER
HERE 204
HEREAFTER 38
HIDE 39
HIGH (dimension) 228
HIGH (prominent) 56
HIGH SCHOOL 22
HILL 151
*HIM
HINDER 196
HIS 234
HISTORY 21
HIT 31
HIT (baseball) 162
HITCH 148
HOE 115
HOG 167
*HOLE
HOLIDAY 79
HOLY 92
HOLY SPIRIT 93
HOME 171 (192, 204)
HOME RUN 162
HOMELY 60
HONEST (-y) 98
HONOR (-ary) 11
HOOK 148
HOPE 53 (207)
HORSE 166, 204

HOSE 115
HOSPITAL 117
HOT 105 (113)
HOT TEMPERED 53
HOUR 73
HOUSE 200
HOW 3 (184, 200, 210, 223, 233)
HOW MUCH MONEY 127
HUG 88
HUMBLE 54
HUMBUG 36
HUMOROUS 50
HUNDRED 82
HUNGER 100
HUNGRY 100
HUNT 165
HURRY 42
HURT 120 (122)
HUSBAND 90
HUSTLING 180
HYPOCRITE 64
HYSTERICAL LAUGH 43

I 1
ICE 103
ICE CREAM 103
ICE SKATE 163
IDEA 12 (232)
IDLE 63
IDOL 169
IF 19
IGNORANT 14
IGNORE 54
ILL (-ness) 118
IMAGINATION 13
IMPART 28
IMPORTANT 65
IMPRESSION 46
IMPROVE (-ment) 30
IN 7 (97, 140, 216, 225, 234)
IN THE FUTURE 78
INCH 86
INCOME 127
INCREASE 126
INDECISION 173
INDEED 25
INDIAN 155 (183)
INDIFFERENCE 52
INDIVIDUAL 131
INDUSTRIOUS 54
INFLUENCE 16
INFORM 15
INJURE 169
INK x
INKWELL x
IN-LAW 91

INNOCENCE 17
INSANE 120
INSANITY 120
INSECT 168
INSIDE 7
INSPECT 137
INSTALL 42
INSTITUTION 22
INSURANCE 126
INTELLIGENCE 12
INTELLIGENT 12
INTENT 15
INTEREST 127
INTERFERE 14
INTERRUPTION 14
INTO 7, 94
INTRODUCE 139
INTRODUCTION 139
INVENTOR 131
INVESTIGATE 137
INVITE 41, 140
IRELAND 154
IRISH 154
IRON (metal) 151
IRON (v.) 111
IT 3
ITALIAN 154
ITALY 154
*IT'S

JAIL 136
*JANUARY
JAPAN (-ese) 155
JEALOUS 43, 54
JELLY 104
JESUS 92
JET 180
JEW (-ish) 156
*JOB
JOIN 138
JOINER 138
JUDGE 19 (158)
JUDGMENT 19, 46
JUMP 159, 229
*JUNE
*JULY
JUST NOW 78
JUST THINK OF IT 214

KANSAS CITY 213
KEEP 129 (197)
KEY 148
KICK 41
KICK OUT 41
KIDDING 190
KIDNEY 119
KILL 137
KIND (-ness) 50

RULE (n.) 48
RULE (v.) 133
RUN 180, 205
RUN (animals) 166
RUN AWAY 37, 137
RUSSIA (-n) 155

SAD (-ness) 49
SAFE 136
SAILOR 134
SALE 127
SALT 102
SAME 91 (224)
SANDWICH 104
SAN FRANCISCO 214
SANTA CLAUS 79 (95)
SATISFIED 103
SATURDAY 76
SAVE 124
SAVE (free) 136
SAVIOR 95
SAW (n.) 116
SAWMILL 152
SAY 55 (170, 204, 219)
SAY! 225
SCALE 86
SCARE 48
SCENT 101
SCHOOL 22
SCOLD 33, 136
SCORE (basketball) 160
SCRAMBLE 30
SCREW DRIVER 116
SEARCH 39
SEAT 112
SECOND (in order) 161, 205
*SECOND (time)
SECONDLY 205
SECRET 39
SECRETARY 130
SEE 55 (145, 191, 200, 229, 232)
SEEK 39
SELECT 18
SELF 2, 3
SELFISH 52
SELL 127
SELLER 133 (127)
SEND (away) 175 (176)
SEND (to me) 28, 175
SENTENCE 21
SEPARATE 42
*SEPTEMBER
SERGEANT 135
SERVE 174
*SERVICE
SEVEN 72

SEVERAL 61 (82)
SEW 111
*SHADE
SHALL 78 (27, 184, 194)
SHAME 48
SHAMEFUL 233
SHARE 32
SHARP 44
SHAVE 113
SHE 1
SHEPHERD 93
SHERIFF 136
SHIP 147
SHOCKED 144
SHOE 132
SHOE REPAIR 132
SHOOT 165
SHORT (-er, -est) 57 (204)
SHORTSTOP 161
SHOT IN THE ARM 117
SHOULD 25 (228)
SHOUT 16
SHOVEL 115
SNOW 15
SHOWER 113
SHUT 139
SHUT UP 180
SHUTOUT 159
SICK 118, 224
SIGN (talk) 29
SIGN YOUR NAME 126
SIGNATURE 126
SILENCE 16
SILLY 47
SILVER 149
SIMILAR 91
SIN 99
SINCE 80
SINK 147
SISTER 90
SISTER-IN-LAW 91
SIT 112 (215)
SIX 72
*SIZE
SKATE, ICE 163
SKATE, ROLLER 163
SKID 68
SKIN 155
SKINNY 178
SKY 94
SLANG TERMS 178
SLAY 137
SLEEP 109 (196)
SLEEPY 109
SLENDER 121
SLICE 103
SLIDE 162
SLIM 121

SLIP AWAY 37
SLIPPER 110
SLOW 42
SMACK (kiss) 182
SMALL (-er, -est) 216
SMART 12
SMELL 101
SMILE 43
SMOKE 106
SMOKER 106
SMOOTH 56
SNAKE 167
SNOW 143
SNUB 54
*SO
SODA POP 105
SOFT 64
SOIL 146
SOLDIER 134
SOME 5 (80)
SOMEONE 5
SOMETHING 5
SOMETIMES 80
SON 89
SONG 20
SORROW (-ful) 49
SORRY 49 (222)
SOUL 92
SOUND 150
SOUND ASLEEP 109
SOUR 101
SOUTH 153 (206)
SOUTH AMERICA 153
SOW 146
SPAIN 154
SPANISH 154
SPEAK 29, 55 (170)
*SPECIAL
SPEECH 55 (170)
SPEECH (lecture) 134
SPELL 197
SPEND 127, 128
SPIDER 168
SPLEEN 112
SPRAIN 121
SPREAD 124
SPREAD (food) 104
SPRING 143
SPRINKLING 115
SPY 217
SQUIRREL 164
STAMP 176
STAND UP 68
STAR 141
START 204
STARVE 100
*STATION
STAY 39

244

Marguerite Bov   La. 7-1198
              14518 Saratoga
Barbara Januszewski   VE-9-1338
      15024 Novara
   Detroit 48205

JACKI STEFFEN 527-3165

Anamae Kirk   PR-3-1531
      19220 Eastland Roseville mich 48066

Judy Ghupido 772-4198
   25885 Dale
   Roseville, Mich. 48066

Mary Mitchell
15820 Croatia
Mt. Clemens. Mich. 48043
      463-9820

Mildred Petrowske
   24354 Dale
   East Detroit, Mi 48021   #771-3317

Betty Pellegrino
31723 Shawn
Warren, Mich. 48093   293-2057